Terror of the Red Pants Attack on Dorchester Road

Nancy Seay

Copyright © 2017 Nancy Seay
All rights reserved
First Edition

PAGE PUBLISHING, INC.
New York, NY

First originally published by Page Publishing, Inc. 2017

ISBN 978-1-63568-630-2 (Paperback)
ISBN 978-1-63568-631-9 (Digital)

Printed in the United States of America

This is a powerful and triumphant story of motivation, faith, and determination. June 28, 1990, I was beaten, robbed, and left for dead. Two hospitals misdiagnosed me as having a sprained collarbone. Two different doctors at two medical centers agreed with them. I was becoming paralyzed, my speech was so slurred, and the left side of my body was limp. They still had no answers for me. Two doctors said that the pain was all in my head and told me to go home and rest.

Finally, after tipping around on my left toes for more than three weeks, I refused to give up. The pain is what kept me moving in search of the truth. And the problem turned out to be that—I had suffered a broken neck during my attack.

For the audience, this book will take its readers on a journey that they can travel to by sitting in their home or in their yards relaxing. After reading one paragraph, they will be hungry for more. This is a fulfilling book. Short but full of food and easy to digest. This book will deliver huge results. Many people will never attend a group session and many will never visit a psychiatrist. This book will serve both and more. There is no age group of people who have been victimized, because victims come in all ages, all races, and all sexes. I expect this book to be a best-seller and a mini movie to be made. I have included at the end a letter to all victims. There is a long shelf life for this type of book because there will always be mistakes made by doctors and there will always be another victim.

Contents

Preface 7
Acknowledgments 12
Acknowledgement 14
Preface 15
Introduction 17
Day of the Attack 20
The First Hospital Visit 27
The Second Hospital Visit 31
The Third Doctor's Visit 35
The Fourth Doctor's Visit 39
The Final Diagnosis 46
Admission into Beth Israel Hospital 51
The Interview with the Reporter 55
The Day of the Surgery 57
The Two Miracles 61
Coming Home from the Hospital 65
My Return to Work 79
The Accident on the Job 100
The Final Episode/Retirement 104
A Message to All Victims of Vicious Crimes and Attacks ... 109
The Statistics of Doctors Errors 111
About the Author 117

Preface

This is not an Alfred Hitchcock creepy novel nor is it a fairytale. This is not something made up just to sell a book. These are actual events that occurred at my place of residence. Although some of the facts are gruesome and painful to write, I must tell the world. This book is long overdue.

I have tried many times over the years to put down in words the events of that day. But it has been too painful for me to write. Although some memories of that day are forever lost, however, the doctors seem to think that is a good thing.

My psychiatrist said that to see my attacker's face would only cause more stress and pain. Therefore, it is good that some of the brain cells did die that day (part of my memory cells). Seeing his face would not help me. In addition, once a person's brain cells die, doctors say that they do not regenerate. In this sense, I consider myself blessed not to be able to put a face on my attacker.

However, the majority of the actual beating will never leave my mind. And since I cannot remember, God knows what is best. My mourning is now over. Only now can I reach back into my mind and pull out all of the painful events of that day. Many times, we do not know how strong our inner person is until we need that extra strength, and then it comes out.

Often, I pretend that my attacker is standing in front of me. I would stand in front of my bathroom mirror and hold a conversation with him. Looking him straight in his face, I tell him that he is forgiven. My therapist tells me that this is the only way I can move on.

I thank God for my therapist because he helped me in many ways with things that I could not do alone. As the years pass by,

I realize that nothing will ever completely take away all the pain, because years later I still have nightmares about the attack.

The doctors call it PTSD (post-traumatic stress disorder). I finally realize that healing is a long and slow process. But with the right type of help, we can live with it. When tragedy hits us in the face, if it does not kill us it will make us stronger.

I know that there is a good reason for my being alive. Any time a tragic event takes place in one's life, one should search for that greater purpose in life. Ask yourself: why was my life spared? The God whom I serve has a purpose for me, and that is why I am here. My belief in God is that he did not save my life just for me to give up, sit down, and die a miserable life.

Although it has been many years coming, putting my attack down on paper has been a kind of therapy for me. I pray that after you have finished reading it, in some way it might be of some help for you, too. Therefore, just remember that whatever you are going through, you are not in it alone.

Sitting here, I realize that it is time to let the world know how a catastrophic incident can turn into a blessing. God allows things to happen to us so that we can look to him for healing and guidance. If we never have any storms in our lives, then how can we ever appreciate the wonders that God bestows in our lives?

I have always felt that since I am a Christian being saved and sanctified, I was exempt from trouble. I knew better, but I just was not afraid of anything or anyone. I was in church services every Sunday, was on many of the auxiliary boards, was very active, and a very good tither.

I did not just go to church, but I lived church. Since the Holy Spirit lived in me, I began to think that I was untouchable. I would say that Satan has no place in my life and that he was no threat to me. However, one thing I had forgotten was the story about Job. Not really forgotten in a sense that it was not there, but I feared no man. Thinking back, this was selfish on my part.

I remember that Job, too, had it all. He had everything any person could ever hope for. This is what my Bible tells me. But one day, Satan came calling. He wanted to test Job's faith in God. As with

TERROR OF THE RED PANTS ATTACK ON DORCHESTER ROAD

Job, God allowed Satan to test me. We will all have our season to be tested. The question is this: when it comes, how will you handle it?

This book is for all of those doubters who believe in God when things are going good for them, when they are happy and never sad, and when they are well and have never faced any type of tragic experience. This book will shake you in a way that you will never forget.

We read about horror movies all the time. We watch them on television. Such things like those in the movies should never happen today with all of the modern technology. This story is long overdue. I should have written it a long time ago. It is essential that people read this book because it will serve as a helpful warning.

Therefore, this book must be published because of the uncertainty of so many families. Families who have lost loved ones with no apparent reason given. Someone told them, "they just died." But the families must follow up on their deaths and get the information through autopsies, if necessary.

The actual events will shock most of the readers. But continue to read because the shocking details will help in many ways you will not believe. This is my true story about the horrible events that took place and how I continue even today to struggle to survive the pain and nightmares. Although my pain is continuous, I have learned not to dwell on it. I try not to think about my past. Therefore not thinking of the pain, I will not pop pills all day. Only when the pain is severe will I take one. Otherwise, I find something to read to try to rid my mind of my pain.

I retired in 1996, after twenty-six years from a communications company. I have since returned back to my home in Birmingham, Alabama.

I wanted this book to be different. I want my readers to feel each word that they read. I left out no details of the events because it is important that people know the type of pain and humiliation I suffered. Not only at the hands of my attacker, but also at the hands of some doctors and some of my managers—the people whom I loved, respected, and looked up to. Also, I did not want to tell the half-truth but the whole truth.

This book, I pray in some way, help other victims who have suffered as I have. This was a triple tragedy but I survived it. By the grace of God, I was able to put my life back in order. The property owner could have prevented this tragedy from occurring. Many complaints to him fell on deaf ears. Because of his negligence and failure to make the necessary repairs to his building, my near fatal attack took place. An intruder entered the building, took my jewelry, my money, and attacked me by breaking my neck and leaving me for dead.

My husband and I had lived in the building for more than twenty years. The attack itself was bad enough. However, the surgery was extensive and very dangerous. The doctors did not know if I would survive the operation or if I would ever walk again. But with great faith and many prayers, I made it through the surgery. I had no doubt because I knew God heard my cry and that I was going to be just fine.

It was more than a month after the attack that I had the surgery. Two hospitals and two doctors misread my x-rays. They misdiagnosed me as having a sprained collarbone. Two doctors even said that the pain was all in my head. But what was driving me insane was that four doctors did not notice the broken neck. That is what made me crazy and I almost lost my mind.

Even when my speech was almost gone and the left side of my body was paralyzed, the doctors still could not give me any reasons for my condition. Therefore, God kept me moving until I found the right doctor who took the time to examine and diagnose my problem. It was finally after much pain, suffering, and many sleepless nights that I made up my mind to visit this fourth doctor again. I said to myself, "He is going to tell me what is wrong with me today. I will just refuse to leave his office and go back home."

I demanded that he take another look at my x-rays. After doing so, he himself was in shock. He said, "I am sending you to see a specialist in this field."

The public has a right to know that many doctors can make mistakes. They have an obligation to treat each patient with the most complete and best care. Therefore, we as patients must be very persistent with doctors. Never let them dismiss you as a crazy person.

TERROR OF THE RED PANTS ATTACK ON DORCHESTER ROAD

No textbook can explain away the pain and suffering that we feel. I am glad that I did not listen to those four doctors. I am glad that I would not give in to my pain. I think the pain was what kept me moving. I was afraid that if I slowed down that I would have stayed down. My legs were barely moving and there was little to no feeling in my left arm.

However, something inside of me said, "Do not stop, keep going, and keep moving forward." I am glad that I did not give up. I knew that had I given up, I would have died and this book would have died with me. My attacker's face is a blur. I only know that he was a black man. This much I remember from when he was following me and when be approached the front door trying to gain entry into the building. I am often amazed, thinking back, that I really want to remember his face. I feel as if I need to see that face once more, and maybe then, I can forget. Once I forget, maybe the nightmares will go away.

When I look at my life now, I love who I am. But do not love how the attack has left me. I have many medical issues because of the surgery which I know was unavoidable. I no longer worry about my speech. I no longer worry about what I can and cannot do. When I am speaking, people look at me in that pitiful way. I have learned to ignore them. I live every day as if it is my last, by never taking anything for granted, then I let tomorrow take care of itself.

I often look back at those days when I was going from doctor to doctor in excruciating pain, knowing something dreadful was wrong, and no one knew but me. If I had not been persistent, and at times pushy, I know in my heart I would be dead today. I will never again allow any doctor ever again to tell me that the pain is "all in your head." I am only alive because I was determined and because I stood up to the fourth doctor.

Therefore, this book will help readers be aware of the many mistakes that are made every day by some doctors who are in too much of a hurry to send you away. My condition is getting worse every day. I pray that this book will be published while I am still able to move around by myself. My attacker suffered no loss. The property owner suffered no loss. The doctors suffered no loss. Therefore, I am the sole sufferer who has lost more than anyone will ever know.

Acknowledgments

Writing this book has provided me a constant reminder of how much I am dependent upon God for all that I attempt to do.

His presence in my life has given me the strength that I need to keep moving forward. I give thanks to him for saving my life and for giving me the faith and the courage not to give up.

Special thanks to my husband Elijah, my best friend, who has supported, comforted, and took excellent care of me. I don't think I could have hired a better caregiver. He never wavered in his duties and his love for me. I will always remember his dedication to me.

I am especially grateful to Dr. J. Noh for his professionalism and his special skills in finding my broken neck. He saved my life and I thank him. I would also like to thank the entire staff of doctors and interns at Beth Israel Medical Center in New York City who committed themselves to my care.

A special thanks to all the nurses who were my caregivers during my stay at Beth Israel Hospital. They treated me as if I was royalty. I will never forget you.

Thanks to Dr. I. Friedman. He was more than my doctor, he was my friend. He made me laugh many times when I wanted to cry. Many thanks to him and his wonderful nurse, Rose.

Thanks to Dr. Stuart Kleinman for he, too, was more than my psychiatrist. He was a mentor to me.

A special thanks to Roxanne, the young woman who accompanied me to the first hospital and stayed with me until the end. I was a stranger to her, but she went above what a stranger would do.

A special thanks to Darlene Bryant and her son Keith, who showed much love.

TERROR OF THE RED PANTS ATTACK ON DORCHESTER ROAD

I owe much gratitude to my parents (my father is deceased). My mom and my pop who rode the Greyhound bus twenty-five hours. They wanted to be there for my surgery. Thank you, mom. You mean the world to me.

Thanks to all my sisters and my brothers from far and near (especially my sister Sadie).

Thanks to my granddaughter Somolia. She was only four years old at the time of my attack. However, she constantly poured out her love to me and this helped to keep me moving forward.

Special thanks to my speech therapist Dr. Sam Chwat, one of New York's finest. Without him teaching me how to speak all over again, I would have been lost. Thank you, again.

Thanks to Ms. M. Pearce from Miles College for first part proofing.

Thanks to Mrs. Shirley Mitchell for her role in my proofing.

Special thanks to Ms. Sonjanika Henderson, my last proof reader.

Special thanks to Coretta Layfield who spent many hours showing me how to work my new computer.

Acknowledgement

I am especially grateful to Kelly Crum, my Publication Coordinator, for her understanding and work with me. Also the editing staff and Page Publishing Company for the work they are doing to help me publish my work.

Preface

Statement of the Author's Purpose

To present the actual facts of a horrific attack and to describe how two major hospitals and two well-known medical centers misdiagnosed a broken neck. This injury, in all likelihood, could have caused my death or could have left me paralyzed for life. However, because of my persistence and unwillingness to give up in spite of all the pain I was in, I would not accept what the doctors said when they told me that "the pain is all in your head." If the pain was all in my head, then why was I becoming paralyzed?

There were no feelings on the left side of my face, my left hand was numb, and my left arm had gone limp. I had to pick it up with my right hand. I knew more than those four doctors knew, and I had no previous training in medicine. However, I had a body that was talking to me and letting me know that something was terribly wrong with it.

The Property owner neglected to make the necessary repairs to his building where I was attacked. The broken elevator had a great effect on my attack because I had to walk up eight flights of stairs, and the attack occurred as I reached the sixth-floor staircase.

I was up and down those stairs more than three weeks after my attack. The doctors said if I had fallen while trying to go up and down during my search for the truth, I would have surely died from my broken neck. Therefore, thanks are to God for he kept holding me up and kept me moving until I discovered the truth.

To inform the public that doctors sometimes make mistakes. Sometimes those mistakes can kill. To tell the world that there is help out there and that help is in this book. How not to give up when you are the only one who knows that you are right. Regardless of who tells you to stop, you need to keep going until you are satisfied.

Just because you are broken, you still have a life. You can live with your brokenness. All you have to do is to have a made-up mind and a determination to keep moving. Do not let any obstacle stand in your way. Push everything aside that is stopping you from reaching your goal.

Therefore by letting people know all about my attack and how today I continue to press forward. I know this book will be an inspiration to all who read it. By putting my story into a book, I am giving people a chance to see me as a person and not just as a victim of a horrific crime. I am a real person who can communicate my feelings to the public.

Introduction

I will never forget how easy it was to fall prey to a horrific attack. I thought I was safe. Then all at once I saw my life changed before me in a matter of seconds. I remember the first feeling that came to my mind that I should have never dismissed.

I was taught that I should always help people who were in need. That it was my duty. Therefore, when I was attacked, I screamed and I yelled but no one came to my rescue. I know someone heard my crying out for help because I was yelling, "Please, God, do not let this man kill me!"

As I think back today, I am still puzzled because I was always helping other people. Never would I turn anyone away. For some mothers on drugs, I was the surrogate mother for many of their children. The children depended on me for clothing, food, and that motherly love. Many times, I would babysit for days not knowing if these mothers would show up.

I never reported any of the parents to Child Protective Services because I did not want the children put in separate foster homes. Therefore, I would take time off from my job and use up some of my personal days and sometimes even my vacation days. I was hoping that the parent would return after a few days, alive and safe.

On one occasion, Ms. Scottie (I will just call her), was high on acid. She went up on the roof of the apartment building. She was threatening to jump off. She kept saying that she saw rainbow colors and that she wanted to jump off and catch them.

Her children were screaming, "Mama, please come down." The oldest child came running upstairs, knocking and crying on my door saying, "Our Mama is on the roof. We need your help." Therefore,

I did what came naturally. I crawl out on the ledge to the fire escape and made my way up to the mother. After talking did not convince her to come down, I grabbed her legs and pulled her back inside the window to safety. I risked my life many times for these misguided mothers and I would do it again because that is who I am.

But when this dreadful attack happened to me, I was expecting someone to come to my aid. I was alone in a lonely cold stairwell screaming for my life. But the tenants stayed inside their apartments. Later after the police arrived, I heard some say that they did not want to get involved and that they were afraid that my attacker could have had a gun. Someone could have called the police, but no one did.

The attack has changed the way I travel. It has made me cautious to the point that I am suspicious of everyone. I never take anything for granted anymore. Life is a precious gift that God has given us. Therefore, we must treasure it always.

I still give to the needy. But there are those who are just lazy and have no desire to work. These types of people do not fall under my definition of helpless.

Four doctors informed me that I had suffered a sprained collarbone from my attack. But they all misdiagnosed my injury. Two even said that the pain was all in my head.

This leads me to believe that overworked doctors sometimes kill. Too many patients and not enough rest are the reasons some of them make enormous mistakes. They do not take enough time with a patient. Sometimes they cannot see what is in front of them (as in my case). How many people have died because of doctors' errors? I am one of the ones who said "look at me again" repeatedly. "Something is dreadfully wrong with me."

We have five senses and an extra spiritual sense that tells us when something is wrong or tells us whenever we are in danger. Many times (like I did), I ignored it. We go about as if we did not hear that voice speaking to us. But we have to learn how to listen when it speaks.

Nobody knows our bodies better than we know them because they are ours. When you know there is something wrong and others tell you that they find nothing or that maybe it is in your head, you must never accept that.

You must keep going until you find the right person (doctor) who can give you the correct information that you need. Many times doctors are too caught up into what they are in. and some are too busy and others might be on drugs themselves (not saying that these four were). Just because doctors have been to medical school does not make them perfect. After all, they are human, and humans do make mistakes sometimes.

These types of mistakes can cause a person to lose his or her life, like the ones who almost cause me to lose mine. Because of four doctors' misdiagnoses, I not only could have died, but could also have been paralyzed from the neck down for life. People, you know your own bodies. Therefore, please listen to it when it is talking to you because our bodies do talk to us and let us know when there is something wrong. However, the key is, we must listen and never ignore the pain. I was one of the fortunate ones who refused to give up. I refused to go home and die without an explanation of why I died.

If you must crawl, I suggest you do that. You must use every means that is available to you, because if you just go home and sit down, there is a probability that you will never get up again.

Many doctors do not get enough sleep. They are overworked and overpaid. Some are busy rushing patients in and out of their offices. Some do not even examine you today. One told me that he promised his wife that he would not touch a female's body. Well, doctor, if you do not touch me, then how can you tell me what my problem is?

Day of the Attack

Let us begin at the beginning. It was a Thursday morning of June 28th, 1990. I was lying in bed, undecided what to do on my off day. Should I stay in bed and rest, or go to my office, pick up my paycheck, and go shopping? I thought maybe I should wait until the next day and shop after work. As I lay there, a small voice said, "Stay in bed and rest today." However, I did not listen. Therefore, after debating an hour, I decided that I would indeed get up.

Thinking that my husband's birthday was in a few more days, I had better shop today. Therefore, I needed to know what my off days for the next week would be. My job schedule came out every Thursday for the following week.

I knew that the Fourth of July would fall two days before his birthday, so I decided I had better shop that day. I jumped out of bed, showered, dressed, hurried down the block, and jumped on the subway.

I arrived on the job about fifteen minutes after nine. I picked up my paycheck and hurried around the corner to Citibank. Even though my job provided a check cashing service on the site, they would not arrive until 10:00 a.m. on paydays. However, I decided not to wait because I wanted to get on the bus and go to the mall. The bank was only five minutes away.

After leaving the bank and hurrying down the block, I waited for the bus. I did not have a long wait. The bus came in about three minutes. I got on and sat in the front behind the driver. The bus ride from downtown took about forty-five minutes.

After arriving at the mall, I went into Richfield's. Richfield's is a men's haberdashery. I had my husband's birthday gift in layaway

TERROR OF THE RED PANTS ATTACK ON DORCHESTER ROAD

there. The salesperson John knew me from previous shopping for my husband. Upon entering the store, John asked me how my husband was doing. He wanted to know if had I come to pick up his gift. Answering him yes, he went into the back of the store, brought the gift out, and asked if he should gift wrap it. I replied, "No, just put it in a large box for me and I will wrap it later at home."

Within minutes, I was back on the bus. Thirty minutes later, I had arrived at my destination. I pulled the cord to inform the driver that I wanted to get off at that stop. He stopped and I exited the bus through the front doors. I went to the grocery store that was halfway down the block. I remember purchasing three items only. But what those items were, I have no idea because it is a blank. I left the store with the large box in one hand and the grocery items in the other.

Just as I approached the corner where I usually walk down the block, I saw a group of men standing there. Past experience had taught me to cross to the other side of the street. These men did not work. They would stand on this particular corner day and night. And when women walked by, they would make unsolicited remarks to them. Since this was such a beautiful day, I did not want to hear any foul language to spoil it. Crossing over to the other side of the road made me feel quite comfortable.

The only thing on my mind was to hurry home and make plans for my husband's birthday celebration. I remembered after checking my schedule that I was posted to work on his special day.

As I walked down the block, a strange feeling came over me. I felt as if someone was following me. It was like I could feel someone breathing on my neck. It was a very daunting feeling, one I had never experienced before. As I turned to look back, I saw a black man wearing a white baseball cap, a short sleeved striped polo shirt, and a pair of red pants. He was walking down the street behind me, close enough to frighten me.

I hurried down the block and walked as fast as I could. I think I was skipping and trying not to inform the man of my fright. I was trying to reach the corner before the light could change because I could see that it was on green. However, before I reached the avenue, the light was red and this caused me to panic.

Feeling uneasy, I started running in and out of traffic. Cars were honking their horns and the drivers were yelling at me to get the hell out of the street. I was almost blind because of fear and because the man was now running, also. It was like I was in a marathon and we were trying to get to the finish line.

Every time I looked back, I could see those red pants getting closer and closer. It had to be no later than 1:30 p.m., and to my surprise, the streets were very crowed for that time of day. So, why was I frightened? I often worked the night shift on my job and get off at midnight.

Usually, when I reach my destination, it was after 1:00 a.m. because the buses and the subways run less frequently at night. Oftentimes, I would have to walk alone at night because no one was going in my direction. I never had a reason to be frightened in all the years that I worked the night shift. But today was different and it was not night. It was in the middle of the day, yet I was afraid and I feared the worse. I just could not shake that feeling.

I lived in a decent neighborhood. A judge lived in the penthouse above my apartment. There were two lawyers on the floor I lived on. Across the street from my building, there lived another judge. Also, a few lawyers lived on my block. Therefore, not much was going on in the neighborhood because there was always police on foot patrol. So I always felt safe walking day and night.

I was thinking that since I had a head start, it would be easy for me to make it to my apartment building. Once I crossed the street, I was only two buildings away, so I thought I was safe. I hurried into the building. The front door had no lock on it, just the inner door. I unlocked the second door. My keys were around my wrist and tied with a red rubber band. This was a habit of mine to keep my keys on a rubber band. I had learned this in a safety meeting some years earlier. When you live in an apartment building, always wear your keys in this manner. This way, you will not have to search in your bag for them.

Hurrying in, I pushed the door closed with my foot because I had packages in both hands. I heard the door click locked behind me. I thought that I was safe and did not have to worry any longer.

TERROR OF THE RED PANTS ATTACK ON DORCHESTER ROAD

But I was wrong, because before I could walk away from the door, the man hurried up to it and pushed on it. But it was locked and he could not get in. He yelled through the door for me to let him in. I told him that I did not know him, and furthermore, we were not allowed to let strangers into this building.

So I walked away. Turning to where the mailboxes were, he then began to ring someone else's bell because I could hear when that person buzzed him in. I stood by the mailboxes and pretended to get mail out of the box. As he entered the door, he stopped where I was standing, and said, "Thanks for not letting me in." He passed by me and proceeded to walk up the three small steps to the hallway and entered the door at the farthest end.

I watched him as the door closed behind him. This door would take you down to the basement or upstairs. I remained by the mailboxes and listened for any sounds. I stood there still, but did not hear him slamming any doors. I was trying to give him enough time to reach wherever he was going.

The mail carrier had left a yellow sticker in my box. The note read, "I left your package with the Super." So, after a few minutes, I finally moved away from the mailboxes. I quietly walked up and rang the super's bell, and when his daughter answered the door, I asked her about my package. She looked, came back, and said that she did not see it. That her father usually put all of the tenants' packages on the table next to the door, but she did not see one with my name on it. She said that I should come back later when her father returned.

I said "thank you" and walked back down the hallway. There was a second stairwell by the elevator that only went upstairs. I entered through this door since I had already seen the stranger take the other staircase which faces the super's apartment. I did not want to run into him again. Walking up, I heard no sounds in the stairway. I thought that just maybe I was wrong about the stranger. Maybe the man in the red pants had come to visit someone else in the building and that he just happened to be walking down the streets at the same time as I was. I thought how silly it was in thinking that this man was following me.

I lived on the eight floor. This was a long walk up those stairs. The elevator had been out of service for more than three weeks. It was out of service more than it was in service. New owners had purchased the building, and all they wanted was the tenants' rent money and barely made any repairs.

I had only reached the sixth floor when I heard a loud bang. It was the door behind me slamming and the man in the red pants was running up the staircase with what appeared to be a pistol in his hand. I was now facing him with a gun pointed in my face. I began to scream, "Oh, my God! Please do not let this man kill me." He put the gun to my head and clicked it, but it did not go off. I knew at that same moment God had heard my cry and saw my tears. However, it was not over yet, for the man put the gun into his belt. I said to him, "Here, take my jewelry. You can have it all. Take my bag. My money is in it, but please do not hurt me." Without saying a word, he lifted my shoulder bag from my shoulders and put it across his shoulders.

What is he dong? I thought that this man must be some kind of a nut, I began to scream louder as I thought he was going to rape me. He was not in a hurry. He was taking too much time. A robber would have taken the money and left. This was really frightening me because I did not know what was next. Was this man angry because I did not let him into the building? What was this man going to do to me? Was he going to kill me or what? In that moment, I saw my whole life flash before me. Why was this happening to me? Haven't I always tried to be a good person? I was always giving to the needy, especially street people. So, why? Then the man said, "Give me the money that is in your bra."

I had already freely given him all the jewelry. Now he demanded the money from my bra. How did he know there was money in my bra? Was he in the bank? I was frightened because he had to have followed me from the bank. However, I did not remember seeing him in the bank. Those red pants would have been a distinguishing mark. The bank was not crowed, and I had taken out what I was going to spend at the mall and the grocery, then put the other into my bra.

I believe he knew because someone had set me up. Maybe someone at the bank told him. I just could not figure out how he would know of the money in my bra. After he had robbed me of my belongings and cash, I thought he would just leave. But instead, he spun me around, grabbed my hair from the back, and pushed my head down into my chest. He started to bang my head into the cement wall. I started to feel like my top teeth were falling out of my head. He then thrust my left shoulder into the wall several times. He was in no hurry for he took his own time hurting me.

My vision blurred. I thought I was almost blind. I was dizzy and could almost feel myself fainting. I was seeing things in triple. The wall was now three instead of one. At that point, I was losing consciousness, and I am sure that if beating had not stopped when it did, I would have died that day.

I barely remembered him picking me up and throwing me down the flight of cement steps. How long I lay there on that cold cement floor unconscious, only God knows. I remember trying to move, but my body just would not comply. I ached with pain all over. Not one part of my body felt well. Oh, how I wished someone would come to my rescue. So many things flashed through my mind. Things like how I should have been more careful of my surroundings. If only I had stayed home that day. All at once, I heard someone ask, "Are you conscious?" I answered, "Yes." But at one time, I must have been unconscious because I cannot remember after he threw me down the stairs as he was leaving.

The man who had come to my rescue was one of the two brothers who lived in the apartment directly under mine. He yelled back upstairs for his brother to come down and help him. I heard him say, "This woman lives upstairs right above us." I was attacked in the sixth-floor stairwell and they lived one floor up. Therefore, they had to have heard me scream. "She has been hurt. Come help me pick her up and take her to one of the neighbor's apartment."

When they found me, they said that I was curled up in a fetal position, and my speech was slurred. They asked me if I was all right, but all I could do was mumble. I tried to get up but could not. All I could do was try to shift my right shoulder and rest on them.

They said that they were on their way to work, or else they would be glad to take me into their apartment. Then I heard a familiar voice that sounded like a friend of my husband's. He was coming down the hallway on the floor where they were picking me up. It was Teddy Lawson, so they called out to him. I nodded for them to take me to his apartment. They told Teddy that I had been robbed and beaten and asked if he would please call 911.

Teddy never said a word, neither a "yes, he would" nor "no." He would not allow them to bring me to his apartment. I could hear him walking back to his apartment. But the brothers rang Teddy's doorbell anyway, and he and his wife Corenda hesitated before they opened the door.

When they finally opened it and I was carried in, I felt a cold chill come over me. I had a funny suspicion that they knew something about the attack and they did not want me in their apartment. Before the brothers could sit me down, Teddy and his wife said to them, "She cannot stay here because we are on our way out." The couple said to the brothers, "Take her downstairs to the super's apartment." As we left their apartment, I thought to myself, "If they were on their way out for the day, then why were they not dressed as if they were on their way out?" I was trying to figure out why they had to leave knowing my condition, and because they were our friends. This couple had visited our apartment on several occasions.

This baffled me: them claiming that they were in such a hurry to leave. They would not wait until the police arrived. They repeated, "Take her down to the first floor and wait in the super's apartment. We have to leave now." It was the way they said it, as if they had not known me before. These brothers were from another country. We were not friends. They had not lived in the building for very long, but they were concerned for me.

Although I was in distress, I managed to tell the brothers to take me to the super's apartment. While waiting for the ambulance and the police to arrive, the owner of the building showed up. Maybe the super had telephoned him during all of the commotion. The super had not come to my rescue, but he had telephoned the building owner. All of this was strange to me because people were out in the hallway on the first floor, whispering and saying, "Oh, that is Ms. Lady who lives upstairs on the eighth floor. We know her."

The First Hospital Visit

The building owner offered to drive me to the hospital because it took the ambulance so long to arrive. There were several calls made from the super's apartment. The police made the last three calls. The police were told that the ambulance was dispatched to another location where the other person's injuries were of a more serious nature than mine were.

A young girl named Roxanne, who was visiting her cousin in the building, volunteered to ride with me to the hospital. Upon arriving at the emergency entrance of the hospital, Roxanne went in and brought back a nurse and a wheelchair. The building owner left us outside the hospital and went on his merry way and did not wait to see the outcome. There were three doctors and four or five nurses all standing around who were watching television and discussing Nelson Mandela's visit to the city the week before.

I sat sobbing and screaming almost two hours and no one came over to me. This made me very angry. I was angry with them because they were professionals standing around talking about Mandela when there were patients who needed their attention. Roxanne finally walked over to them, "Why are you laughing and having a good time when this women has been sitting here in pain and screaming?" Roxanne got their attention because a nurse came over and asked me, "What happened to you, and why are you so hyperactive?" Before I could answer her, Roxanne spoke up, "This woman has been attacked and was left for dead. You are not showing any concern for her."

The nurse tried to calm Roxanne down, but she kept on talking. She then asked me if I could tell her what my chief complaint was. I tried to explain in detail what had occurred, but the nurse stopped writing. She said, "I have enough information." Then proceeded to take my blood pressure and temperature. The nurse said, "Your temperature is good. But due to your hysteria, the blood pressure is extremely high."

The nurse then beckoned a doctor to come over. He came and took a quick look at the chart, looked me directly in my eyes, and asked, "Did the man rape you?" I responded, "Why would you ask such a question? Do you see any talk about a rape there on that chart?"

The doctor said, "I see here that he put a gun to your head. In many of these cases, they usually rape their victims."

His comments made me furious. He then asked me to lift up my left arm, but it was too painful to try to move it. I finished explaining to him about how my attacker had banged my head into the cement wall several times and slammed my left shoulder into the cement wall several times as well. After that is when this feeling of numbness and tingling in my left arm started. The pain then went down the left leg to my foot. My forehead began to hurt awfully.

I asked the doctor what could have caused my speech to be almost incoherent. He said, "I am sending you for some x-rays and then I can tell you something more definite." The technician came and pushed me into the x-ray room. He explained to me that I would have to stand up for the tests.

Barely standing and almost leaning over, I managed to get out of the chair and stand. Soon after I stood, I could feel him pressing himself into my rear end. I pushed him away from me with my elbow. However, he tried it again. This time I could feel his penis hard against my bottom. I elbowed him again much harder than before. He finally stopped molesting me. I will never forget how he abused me in my terrible condition. I could not walk and could just barely able to stand, but he was not concerned. He just wanted to get a good feeling rubbing up against me.

This occurred only because I was in no position to defend myself. If I had been able to fight both of these men off me, I would have. Being attacked twice in one day, first by a black man and then by a white, was unbelievable. The man finally finished the last set of x-rays and instructed me to sit in the chair outside the x-ray room until someone came to take me back. A nurse came about ten minutes later and wheeled me back around the corridor. The doctor came back after about another hour, and holding the films up to the light, he said, "I see no broken bones. You have only soft tissue injuries as far as I can see."

I asked him, "Just what does that mean? Does that type of injury make your left side paralyzed and your speech bad? Does it make pain run up and down your left leg to your foot? What about the head injury?"

He said, "I checked your eyes and there is no redness or blood in them. Your head is hurting because of the knocks to it. There is nothing to worry about there. You do have a sprained collarbone." He then said, "Sometimes, a soft tissue injury can cause severe pain in different parts of a person's body."

I asked him again if a sprained collarbone could cause my speech to get bad. He did not answer me. He just wrote a prescription for pain pills, put my arm in a sling, and sent me home, saying, "I hope you feel better soon." Not once did he lay me on the table and examine me. Roxanne went outside and flagged a taxi to take us back home.

When we arrived back at the apartment building, I sat in the taxi just staring at the building. I was too afraid to enter it again. It was as if I was frozen and could not move. The taxi driver kept saying, "That will be six dollars, please." He repeated six dollars over again, but all I could do was sit and stare out the window at the building. Roxanne was looking at me. My husband had been talking to some people in front of our building, and he walked over and paid the driver the six dollars. I hugged and thanked Roxanne for all of her kindness. Someone had told my husband about the attack when he arrived home from work.

He asked the super to help him get me out of the cab. They picked me up and carried me upstairs to our apartment. Inside our apartment, he thanked the super for all his help. He said, "you are welcome." And left the apartment. My husband gave me a bath and then put me to bed. He kept asking what happened and why I had not called his job. He said that he had heard the super's version of it. However, he did not know all the details. Therefore, I started pouring out my heart to him. It was hard for him to understand me. He got very angry. In all the years we had been married, I had never seen him this angry.

The look that was on his face that night, I pray I will never see again. It sent chills through me because I knew he wanted to kill this man. He wanted to know what the attacker looked like and how did he sound. My husband was an officer and he was getting ready to launch his own attack. He grabbed his service revolver and put some extra bullets in his pocket. He kept saying over and over how this was a senseless attack because the man had taken my money and the jewelry and did not have to hurt me the way he had. I was a small-framed woman weighing not even a hundred and fifteen pounds. Seeing the anger in my husband's eyes and his voice, I said, "Enough talking for now."

Trying to lie down was very painful. He tried putting pillows under me, but they did not help for the pain was severe. He started to rub me to try to help ease the pain, but that did not work. He even brought a hot bottle of water and laid it close to my neck, but to no avail. I told my husband to dial 911 because I needed to go back to the hospital. He was slow in doing so, but I was not going to argue with him. He got me ready and then dialed 911. A few minutes later, they arrived and carried me in a wheelchair down eight flights of stairs.

The Second Hospital Visit

Before we drove off, the attendants said that they were taking me to another hospital. When they carried me into the emergency room, it was very crowed. The nurse told us they had to treat the inmates first. If other patients were not bleeding or having a heart attack, then the inmates took priority due to the Correctional Officers' time line. Therefore, we would have to wait since they saw no blood on my body, which meant no serious injuries. They considered blood to be more serious unless I was having a heart attack. Not knowing my condition, they had no way of knowing how serious my injuries were.

After hearing the nurse's statement, the ambulance attendants left me sitting there in a wheelchair. I kept counting the inmates. Fifteen were before me. Later, more kept coming in. It seemed as if they would never stop coming. I had not seen that many prisoners in one setting except the ones in movies on the television.

Finally, after waiting almost four hours, the time was three-thirty, Friday morning on June 29th. A nurse came over and asked what was the problem. I was trying to explain. However, my speech was now worse than before. She took my blood pressure and temperature. She told me that my blood pressure was extremely higher than normal. She went on filling out the chart and asking me for more details. I was not able to explain to her as much detail by detail, but I had brought with me the discharge paper from the first hospital visit. I had begun to sob and scream because of all the pain I was in. The nurse said that a doctor would be with me shortly.

However, I had to wait another two hours before the doctor, Dr. Willie, finally came. His first question was, "Why are you wearing that brace on your arm?" I made a gesture for him to give me a pen and paper, so I could try and write the answers down. "Look at the paper on my chart from the first hospital." I was trying to explain how the first hospital had put it on me. He then asked me what the first hospital said about my injuries. Again, I wrote that the doctor had said that I had a sprained collarbone and that all I had was only soft tissue injuries.

Doctor Willie was speaking to me while sitting on a chair and was explaining to me that they had no examination rooms to examine me in. That they were full to capacity with other patients. I tried to explain all the different ailments to him expecting the doctor to say, "Let me take a look and examine you myself." I went on to explain how my speech was almost gone. However, the doctor's only words were, "Take this referral down the hall to the x-ray department, and wait there until someone calls your name."

It was now daylight outside and the sun was bright. The night shift had left. Therefore, my x-rays were done quickly. This time, they did take the time to x-ray my knees, neck, and head. My knees were badly bruised from the man throwing me down those steps, I suppose, because I do not remember him hitting me on them. After all of the tests, I was sent back down the hall to see the doctor. He came back into the hallway where I was sitting, and said, "They still have no rooms for me to examine you in." He further said that he saw nothing new that would suggest that the first doctor's diagnosis was not correct. It looked to him like it was a sprained collarbone. He put some iodine on my knees, gave me a prescription, and said that I should follow up in a few days with my primary physician.

Before I left the hospital at five-thirty, Friday morning on June 29th, I telephoned my husband from the lobby to inform him I was waiting on a taxi to bring me home. He asked me what the hospital said about my injuries. I tried explaining that the doctor said just what the first hospital had said. He said, "Baby, two different doctors cannot be wrong. Maybe it is just a sprain and nothing more." He said that he was getting dressed for work, and that I should come on home and try to relax.

TERROR OF THE RED PANTS ATTACK ON DORCHESTER ROAD

I was still waiting in the lobby when Black Pearl car service driver came up and asked if I had called for a cab. I responded, "Yes." He helped me into the taxi, and about five-fifty, I arrived back at the apartment building. The taxi stopped. I was still sitting with tears in my eyes. The driver turned to me and asked if there was anything he could do for me. I was so dismayed after leaving yet another hospital with no one having explained to me any reason for my current condition. I thought that maybe a stranger listening would have had an objective opinion. Therefore, I started trying to explain to him my situation. The driver was very sympathetic to my pain and injuries. He listened carefully and patiently and never once interrupted me.

Finally, when I paused, he started to talk. He told me how brave he thought I was. He also agreed with me that there was something else terribly wrong with me that the doctors had just overlooked. He then said to me, "Lady, you have lost enough already. You owe me nothing." He then helped me out of the taxi and waited until I had unlocked the door and gone inside the building. As I watched him drive off, I wished he had given me his name so that I could thank him for his kindness. The pain was unbearable. However, the stranger's view meant a lot to me. It made me know that I had to keep on looking for the right answers.

Struggling to get up the three steps in order to get to the main floor, I tipped on my left toes to the super's apartment. I rang his doorbell because I needed help in climbing the stairs and knew that I was afraid to try to climb by myself. Every time I entered the building, it was replaying the whole attack over again in my bead. A sinister feeling came over me that sent shock waves through my body.

The super was polite and still very apologetic to me concerning the attack. He helped me up the stairs and waited until I was safe inside the apartment. I locked myself in and crawled from the living room down the hallway to my bedroom. I had crawled as far as I could, but could not get into my bed. Eventually, I did fall asleep on the bedroom floor.

My husband arrived home from work and thought I had fallen out of bed. However, I explained that my legs hurt too badly to try to lift them up into the bed. Several times during that night, I woke up screaming from the nightmares. The next morning, my husband could not understand anything that I was trying to say. My speech had gotten worse than the day before, and the only words coming out of my mouth were gibberish and scrambled words. I could no longer stand on either leg. Therefore, my husband had to carry me up and down the stairs.

I asked him to call my job and explain to them the circumstances. "Tell them that you have no idea when I will be able to return to work. Tell them to put me out on sick pay." I was not able to speak for myself, only able to scribble down on paper what I wanted to say. Being a lefty, the scribbling with my right hand was not very legible. But my husband managed to read what I had written enough to explain to my job the situation I was in.

Another week had now passed and my condition grew worse each day. I knew that someone had to find the problem and fix it quickly. My constant complaining irritated my husband. He did not know how much pain I was in or how I was suffering. The doctors were looking at me but not seeing me. I was a terrible mess and they were overlooking the signs that were in front of them. They were so convinced that I was a nut case because of my attack, and this caused them to not see what was apparent.

The Third Doctor's Visit

After a few hours of sleep, the pain intensified. I could not lay on my back or either side. Once again, I asked my husband if he could take me to another hospital. He said maybe I should just take a pain pill and lie down for a while and maybe I would feel better once I woke up.

I refused to take another pain pill or go back to sleep because I did not want to be dependent on those pills. He decided that it would be best for him to take me to see someone else. He got me dressed and carried me around the corner to our neighborhood health center. This center was in walking distance to our apartment, so I leaned on him and tipped on my toes the few blocks.

Upon arrival at the center, the receptionist asked what was the problem. She could not understand anything I was trying to say. She gave me a pen and paper to write with, but my scribble was so bad, so she turned to my husband and asked him to tell her what was my problem.

My husband explained to her that I had been attacked and told her what the two other doctor had said. He told her that my condition had worsened and that he needed to find out why his wife was getting worse. The nurse asked if we have any of the x-rays from either of the two hospitals. I nodded no and showed her the emergency room discharge paper that I had on me. She pointed to an open door and said for me to go in it and that Doctor Maxie would be with me shortly.

A few minutes later, Doctor Maxie walked in and said that he would need to see the x-rays from the previous hospital and that it would be best if he could view the first hospital tests. After a very brief examination, he said maybe some of my pain might be all in my head because of the severity of the attack. He also said he would call the hospital and request my x-rays. Once he gets the x-rays, he would call me back in.

After we arrived back home, I decided that I needed to take a pain pill and lie down. I could feel an anxiety attack coming on, and I did not want to burden my husband any more that day. So I took one pain pill and a sleeping pill. I fell off to sleep quick, because the next thing I knew, my husband was waking me, saying, "Dinner is ready."

I tried to turn over on my side to eat, but I was in too much pain. Finally, he came around to the other side of the bed and propped me up. He put the bib around my neck and proceeded to feed me. The left side of my face was paralyzed and the food dripped down on my chin onto my gown. Therefore, the bib was necessary. This entire experience of my husband spoon-feeding me began to cause me to feel like a baby again.

After my meal, he picked me up like a little baby and carried me into the bathroom. He put me in a warm tub of bubble bath and let me relax in it for a while. Finally, after about fifteen minutes the water was getting cool, so he came and after drying me off, put a clean gown on me and put me to bed for the night. I could not sleep because, every time I would close my eyes, those red pants were there.

Once and for all, I did go off to sleep because it was morning the next time I opened my eyes, and my husband was dressing for work. There was just enough time to feed me, but I could not eat because my mouth felt as if it were twisted. So as he was bathing me, I looked up at him, and said, "I need to see another doctor."

But he said, "Maybe you need to take the other doctor's advice, and wait until he receives the x-rays from the first hospital. Maybe some of your pain could be all in your head like the doctor said."

This pissed me off, because he knew from watching me every day that something was seriously wrong. He saw the changes taking place in my body every day. That there was something else wrong with me. I stopped listening to him because he was only repeating what he had heard Doctor Maxie say.

TERROR OF THE RED PANTS ATTACK ON DORCHESTER ROAD

I was angry at him for saying such a thing to me, and was glad that he was on his way out the door. It was good for him that he had to go to work, because I might have said something that I probably would have regretted. Before he left, he tried to kiss me good day but I turned my face from his. He knew I was angry because I always kissed him before he left the house. But this time was different. So he left the apartment saying, "I'll call you later."

After he closed the door and I heard the locks click, I screamed and moaned. I could not figure out why he would even say such a thing to me. I really felt helpless now because all I could do was just lie there. I could not do anything for myself, not even feed myself.

I looked down at my breakfast that he had left on the bed beside me. It had gotten cold by now. But I did manage to use my right hand to pick up some of the food, but I had a hard time trying to chew it. The food kept running down on the side of my face to my chin. My gown had more food on it than was on the plate.

Hours had passed and I heard the locks click on the front door. I was happy to hear him come in, because the telephone had not rung that day. As I tried to put a smile on my face, he walked into the bedroom with a McDonald's bag in his hand. He said that he had had a long and stressful day on the job. That he was too tired to cook so he just stopped at the first fast food place he saw. He asked me if I was hungry or if I want him to go back out and get me something else for dinner.

I said that the happy meal was just fine and could he please take me to my bathroom because I had not been all day. He did as I asked, and gave me my bath while we were in the bathroom. I was getting ready to have the conversation again about going to see another doctor, but the telephone rang.

The voice on the other end said, "This is Ms. Hopper. I am the nurse calling from your job's medical department. Dr. Shelley has scheduled you for an appointment with her for this Friday at 9:30 a.m. It is important that you keep this appointment because your sick pay depends on you keeping it. You are to come up to the third floor in the main building. We will send a car service to pick you up at nine o'clock. We will see you then, okay?" I said, "I'll see you on Friday at 9:30 a.m."

I told my husband that since today is Tuesday, I will try to hold out from seeing a new doctor until I see the company's doctor on Friday. He thought that was a good idea, because he did not want to go anyway. That night was quiet in the apartment because neither one of was talking. He as watching television in the living room and I was reading my Bible in bed.

I must have fallen asleep because I don't remember when he came to bed. About three-thirty the next morning, I had to go to the bathroom, so I nudged him and he helped me out of bed. I could not get back to sleep, so I read a few more scriptures.

He got up, made breakfast, fed me, and asked if I wanted my bath now. I said, "Not now, just let me finish reading." As he put me in the bathroom, I began to cry again. All I could do was think about Friday morning.

The Fourth Doctor's Visit

We know our bodies better than anyone else does, and when something is wrong, we are the first to know it even when doctors cannot find the answers that you so badly need. Moreover, when they do not take the time to further investigate your complaint, that's when you know it is time for you to seek help someplace else. What makes them qualified to tell you that your pain is all in your head?

When they have failed to fully investigate all probabilities, what gives them the right to call a person crazy? Whenever you are in doubt, do not let them write you a prescription and send you away. Always be watchful and careful who you accept advice from.

The next few days went by fast because I was thinking about the company's doctor. I had already written the questions down on paper that I wanted to ask her. I thought that since I was an employee of theirs, they would be more than eager to help me find the answers that I was so in need of. I was counting on them to help relieve some of my fear, if not all.

Early Friday morning, my husband got me fed and dressed, and we waited for the car service. About eight-thirty, my doorbell rang. The voice on the other end said, "My name is Juan. I was sent to pick you up to take you to your company's doctor's appointment. Can you come down please?"

My husband said to the man that we will be right down in about five minutes and could he please wait. Coming and going up and down those eight flights of stairs was getting harder to do. I was putting all of my weight on my husband, and he was struggling with me daily. We finally made it downstairs and out to the waiting car service.

It takes about twenty minutes from the apartment to the company's medical building. This building houses several different floors. The cafeteria is on the first floor near the security guard's desk. Several other offices are on other floors. We arrived about eight-fifty in front of the building. Before we exited the car, the driver said, "The nurse always calls for me fifteen minutes before you are to leave. So I will be right here waiting for you when you come out."

As I entered the building, the security guard stopped me at the front desk and asked for my ID card, telling me that I had to sign in also. I said, "No problem." After I showed my ID and signed in, he then called upstairs to announce that my husband and I were on our way up.

When we reached the third floor, the receptionist told us to have a seat and that Dr. Shelley would be with us shortly. Minutes later, I was told to go into a certain room and wait there. The nurse told my husband that he had to wait in the waiting room for me.

A few minutes later, the doctor entered the room. She was a small-framed young female. She looked to be thirty or younger. She looked at me, and said, "Did you bring your x-rays with you?" I said, "No, because I do not have them and you did not request that I bring them with me." She then says, "Without those films, there isn't much that I can do for you today."

I tried to show her my note with the questions that I had scribbled down. But all she said was, "You need to go back to the medical center and get a copy from them." I told her that I was not able to run from place to place trying to get copies of my films. That it would be faster and best for her if she requested them and have a messenger service deliver them. The medical center is waiting on a copy themselves.

She said, "Thank you for that advice, and as soon as I receive the films, I'll call you back in again." She said, "Good-bye and have a nice day."

Was she some kind of a fool? How could I have a nice day in my present condition. She could have kept her cliché to herself. What a dumb thing to say.

TERROR OF THE RED PANTS ATTACK ON DORCHESTER ROAD

She did not ask me how was I feeling or coping since the attack. She seemed to only be interested in those films. To me, this visit was a waste of my time and hers. I believe she wanted to look at me and determine from looking what type of condition I was in. There could be no other reason for the visit.

We left the office and when we came out of the building, the car service was there waiting on us. Juan said, "The nurse called me. I was still in the vicinity. How do you feel now, Ms. Lady?" I said, "I'm in a lot of pain and I'm disappointed." I dared not say anymore because that particular car service had a contract with the company.

Therefore, I knew not to say too much to him. He drove slowly on the way back and asked if I need to make a stop before I reached home. I said, "No, thank you anyway, for asking." We arrived back home in twenty minutes. We were let out in front of the building. I was glad there was a parking space so I would not have to walk down the block to the building.

After we made it safe inside the apartment, I then started to discuss with my husband what the doctor had said. I told him how she would not let me ask her any questions and how cold she was to me. She was not very professional for a doctor. I think she was one of those medical students who did not qualify for her degree, so she was hired by the company instead.

Being exhausted, I just wanted to take a pill and lie down for a while, and that is exactly what I did. My husband undressed me and gave me a pill and put me to bed. Soon, I was sleep. Later, my husband woke me with a lunch tray by my bedside. He cleaned me up and gave me lunch.

Another week had passed and I had heard nothing from either doctor. I asked my husband to call and see if they had received my films or not? He called both doctors and both said that they had not received them yet, but were still waiting on them and for me to just be patient.

Two more days passed. I told my husband to get me dressed and take me around the corner to the medical center. I said, "I don't want to wait another day. I need some answers today and I refuse to wait longer." My husband started to say something but he changed his mind.

He said "Okay, I'll get you dressed and we'll go and see what the doctor has to say." My mind was made up. I was not going to argue with him because I was going even if I had to crawl down eight flights of steps and crawl all the way to the medical center by myself.

My head was clear of what I had in mind to do. I was going to go into the doctor's office and just refuse to go home until he tells me what was wrong with me. I knew I was not able to lay on his floor, but I was going to sit in a chair and not let anyone move me. I was going to show him how a crazy person really acts, since he had said that some of the pain was all in my head. Well today, he would see me in action.

When we arrived at the doctor's office, his receptionist asked if I have an appointment. I said, "No, I do not, but I'm here to see the doctor. I have been waiting on a call from you all but have not received one." Before, she claimed that she could not understand me, but now she understood my gibberish perfectly.

The doctor called me into the office. He said, "I looked at the films while you were waiting, and I see nothing new to report to you. What the two other doctors said is probably correct because I see no broken bones. Like I told you before, some of your pain is in your head. I'm going to write you a prescription for some anxiety medication. This will help with the sleeping pills. Now go home and get some rest, and you will soon start to feel better once this medication gets into your system."

I left his office disappointed again, because I knew all of the doctors had misread my x-rays. This was the fifth visit: the second time I had seen him, the two hospitals, and the company doctor. And still, no reasons are given why I am without the use of my limbs and my speech is awful. Tears were streaming down my face and I could not control my crying out loud. People were watching me as they passed by, but I could not help myself. I needed someone to hear me and to take notice of me. I was not giving up. I was determined to be heard.

TERROR OF THE RED PANTS ATTACK ON DORCHESTER ROAD

We finally made it back to the apartment. My husband again put me to bed, and he went out to buy dinner for the two of us and to have my new prescription filled. I was in shock. I just could not believe the doctor saw no broken bones. Something had to be broken, or else why was half of my body limp?

As I lay in bed that night, I had a plan in mind. I dare not discuss it with my husband because he saw me but did not see me. Tomorrow, I was going back to the center and I was going to get some results this time around.

My husband got dressed for work, kissed me good night, and said that he would call to check on me on his lunch break. So, he left for the night. I laid there awake and afraid to go to sleep most nights that he worked. But tonight was different. Although I was afraid to sleep, I was planning for the following day.

The next morning, my husband came in with breakfast in hand. I said that he could rest and that I was not too hungry right then. After he got some rest, I needed to talk to him. He took a nap, and when he woke, I told him my plans. He was too tired to argue with me, so he said, "All right. After you eat, we will go back to the center."

I staggered into the center with my husband holding me up. The receptionist looked at me and asked if I have an appointment because they had just seen me yesterday. I said, "No, but I want to see the doctor." She could not say another word. I sat down in a chair and looked at her rolling my eyes back and forth. I think I frightened my husband because he said nothing. He just looked at me and then he sat down. I was stressing myself out, but I needed some answers because my condition was worsening.

Something was wrong and I knew it, but the doctors did not seem to care. They were in good health and going on with their lives, but my life was at a standstill. I could not even sit on the commode by myself or go to the bathroom without assistance. I was being fed like a newborn baby with food drooling down from my mouth. Today, I was not leaving without some answers as to what was wrong with me.

I said, "Tell the doctor that I am back and I am not leaving here until he looks at my x-rays again." I know this was a bold move, but I had no choice because I knew they were overlooking something. The receptionist walked past me without looking at me, and went in the doctor's office and closed the door.

She came back out and said that he was seeing another patient, but as soon as he had some free time he would call me back. I waited almost an hour and he finally called me into his office. Before he could open his mouth, I managed to get out, "There is nothing wrong with my mind but there is something wrong with my body. It is not my shoulder nor is it my collarbone. You are my primary doctor and you have been treating me for years. Do I sound like an irrational person? Have you ever known me to act in such a manner? Now, Doctor, I need for you to take another look at my x-rays."

Therefore, the doctor looked at them again. This time, he put them up against a wall light and took them down and put them back up again. He left out of his office and went into another room. I could hear him. He was very emotional. I heard him say, "I am sending you a patient right away. This is an extreme emergency. She might have something broken. I will call you as soon as we put her in a cab and send her to you."

After the doctor hung the telephone up, he walked out of his office and said, "I am sending you to Manhattan to see a specialist. He will examine you further and make the determination on what course of action to take next."

I said, "Doctor, what did the x-rays show? What is wrong with me?" All he said was, "I cannot tell you anymore right now. The specialist will explain everything to you when he sees you."

He told his nurse to call a taxi for me and to give him the address where he was to take me. He gave the films to my husband, and said, "I am so sorry. Your wife was right and we were wrong." He told the taxi driver to drive safe and to not hit any bumps. His nurse gave the driver a voucher, and said, "The doctor is expecting you."

The nurse then turned to me, and said, "The doctor is expecting you. I am sorry, also." As we got into the taxi, the doctor and nurse who were standing in the door way said again, "I am so sorry. I wish you all the luck." I looked back at him before the car drove away, and asked him again, "What is wrong with me?" (The center was a walk-in with just one floor that led out to the streets). The

TERROR OF THE RED PANTS ATTACK ON DORCHESTER ROAD

doctor just repeated, "The surgeon will explain everything to you. Go now, driver."

All along, I knew something was wrong with me, but the doctors did not. A person does not have to be a genius to realize when they lose their speech and one side of their body has gone limp that they do not have a sprained anything. That just was not possible. Furthermore, I was not crazy.

Now thinking back, some of the doctors might have been in the business too long. Maybe it was time for them to retire instead of still treating patients, because there comes a time when you can no longer do your job. It is time to step aside and let some fresh minds take over.

The Final Diagnosis

The doctor's office was in lower Manhattan. It was a very short ride across the Manhattan Bridge. We arrived about fifteen minutes later. When we entered his office, he introduced himself as Dr. Noh and that doctor Mandy had already given him details. He said, "Therefore, you do not have to try to repeat it to me. I need you to go with my nurse behind those curtains. She will help you get undressed. She will let me know when you are ready. Then I will come in and do my own examination of you."

After she had finished helping me get undressed, she called for the doctor to come into the room. I remember as if it was just yesterday. He ran his hand down my neck and back, then up my neck again. He then asked my husband, "How long has she been walking around like this?" The doctor then called in a technician and told her to take only one-x-ray. After she finished the test, she said, "I'd like for you to wait outside my office."

A few minutes later, she came running out of the lab and passed by me with her head down. Although she had not looked at me, I knew something was dreadfully wrong.

The look on her face—she looked frightened. This gave me confirmation: the answer I had so long sought. Something terrible was wrong with me. The answers that I wanted to hear were now staring me in the face. I had been searching for the truth, and now I was frightened more than ever because I was now about to learn my fate.

God had kept me alive so that I could meet Dr. Noh. The technician walked into the doctor's office and slammed the door behind her. I could not hear all of the conversation because the door was closed. However, I heard enough shouts to know that I was about to hear some very bad news. Minutes later, the nurse walked out of the doctor's office. She had the strangest look on her face as if she felt sorry for me.

My legs began to shake right there in my seat because I knew that the news was not good. All at once, I began to shake all over as if I was having a seizure or something. I could not control the shaking and even my head began bobbing. The doctor came to the door and beckoned for my husband and I to come in. Almost immediately, he started rambling off, almost stammering worse than I was. He told us that my neck had been broken during the attack some weeks earlier.

I said, "Do you mean that all these weeks I have been walking around with a broken neck, and that is why I am going paralyzed?"

The doctor then asked my husband, "How in God's name has she endured all of this pain for so long? Who helped her get around like this?" My husband said, "She had been sliding around with the help of others and myself most of the time." The doctor then said, "She is lucky to be alive after all these weeks. Your wife's neck is broken and is disconnected from her spine.

"The bone is almost through her back." He then asked my husband and I to step outside while he made a few telephone calls. My legs could not move. They felt like someone had glued them to the floor. My husband and I were both in shock because it took all these weeks for the two of us to find out the truth. I knew that something was broken somewhere.

The doctor had to say a second time, "Would you please step outside? Please." I managed to put one foot in front of the other and exited his office. I could hear him speaking almost incoherent at times to someone on the telephone. He was saying that he had to admit a new patient into the hospital right away. He said, "I need a bed ready for her for Monday morning." I could not hear all what was being said, yet I knew I was getting ready to be admitted into the hospital. I could hear the angry tone in the doctor's voice because I heard him say, "No, this cannot wait. Find a bed for her."

The technician must have told someone about my condition because the other nurses and attendants were peeping from around the corner at me. I could hear their whispers, "She is still alive after all these weeks. Just look at her."

The doctor finally came out of his office with admiration in his eyes. He was still saying, "I really do not know how you walked around in all this pain. I just cannot figure out how you withstood the pain. It is a wonder you had not fallen down those eight flights of stairs going back and forth and going from doctor to doctor over three weeks' time. You are a miracle. If you had fallen down the stairs in that condition, you surely would have died or would have been paralyzed for life. Woman, you are so very lucky."

I said, "Doctor Noh, luck had nothing to do with it. God's grace kept me going and kept me strong until I found the right answers. I had prayed to God that the answers would come soon, because my condition had worsened and I was getting weaker. I did not know how much longer I could keep tipping around on my toes before I did fall down. So, it wasn't luck. It was a blessing from God because he always looks out for his own."

He called his nurse, Mary, back into the office and told her that they had a bed ready for me on Monday morning at Beth Israel Hospital. He told her to check his patient list, and if there were no life-threatening ones, to schedule me for surgery for one day next week.

His nurse told me to report to the hospital on Monday morning since it was now late Friday evening. She gave me my admission papers, and said, "The doctor would meet you there at the hospital." She called a car service to take my husband and I back home.

After returning home, my husband started to pack a bag for me. I was angry. I don't know who I was angrier at: my attacker or those four doctors I had seen. I felt betrayed, as if this was another attack on me. Why had not these two hospitals and those two medical centers found the broken neck and to tell me that the "pain was all in my head?"

After settling down, I asked my husband to dial my parents' telephone number for me. My mom answered the phone. I informed her what the doctor had said and also about my pending surgery. My mom said, "Hang up the telephone. Do not try to talk anymore.

TERROR OF THE RED PANTS ATTACK ON DORCHESTER ROAD

Your father and I will be there. I am going to start packing now. We will be in New York sometime tomorrow night. We will be taking the first Greyhound bus that's leaving tonight. Your father will not fly. You know he is afraid of airplanes."

I thought that maybe I had heard my mom wrong when she said "your father and I" because my father, in all of his seventy-one years, had never left the State of Alabama. Through all of my pain and trials, I felt good because my parents had children spread out all over the states and Pop had never visited any of them.

However, my mom had visited many times before. She had visited all of her children. I redialed my mom's number again, "Mom, did I hear you right? Pop is coming, too?" She said, "Yes, he is." When I hung up the telephone, my husband started to cry.

He said, "You told me that something else was wrong with you. I am so sorry I did not believe you. Can you ever forgive me? Now I understand why you are in so much pain and why the pain pills are not working."

He was just as horrified as I was. He said, "This is like a nightmare. Things like this just do not happen today with all of this modern technology. There is no way so many doctors should have missed a broken neck." My husband was upset and it was hard for me to calm him down, because at one point, he thought that the doctors were right and that the pain was all in my head. We talked all night. Both of us were too angry to sleep that night.

Early the next morning, the telephone started to ring off the hook. Mom had called the other family members. They were all concerned and worried about me. I appreciated the attention, but was not in the mood for all of the questions they were asking me.

People really do mean well, but sometimes they do not know what to say to comfort a person. Sometimes it is just best to listen and not try giving an injured person advice. People cannot tell you how you are supposed to be feeling, nor can they tell you how you should feel.

Sunday was a quiet day. Only a few calls came in. My husband had already cooked breakfast when he came into the bedroom to wake me. He gave me a bath after we finished eating. He also did some house cleaning and left me to read my scripture for the day. I started to scream out in pain. He came running into the bedroom to ask what was wrong. I explained that I was in a lot of pain. He gave me two pills and I fell off to sleep. He later woke me and said that he had went out and brought back dinner and if I was ready to eat. I said yes.

After I finished eating, he had to wash me and put me on a clean gown, because I had drool all over the top of the one I had on. Since there was no feeling on the left side of my face, food would dribble down.

It was hard falling asleep that night, because every time I closed my eyes, the nightmares just kept coming back. The sleeping pills did not help that night. Although my eyes were heavy, sleep just did not come. Maybe it was fear that had built up in my mind. Sometimes fear is more powerful than sleep is.

Admission into Beth Israel Hospital

It is now Monday morning. We have arrived at the hospital's admissions office. I am frightened because I do not know what to expect. Even though the surgeon had already explained some of the procedures to me, I was still frightened because there are so many doubts in my head. All of the explaining cannot take away my fear of the unknown.

The admissions nurse directed my husband and I down a long hallway. She explained, "You would have to go for new x-rays and a CAT scan. In addition, when you are finished there, you have to go for additional tests that are required for admission. An EKG and then some blood work." She said that an attendant would come and take me for the CAT scan.

It took about ninety-minutes for all of my pre-admission testing to be completed. Finally, I was escorted upstairs to a semi-private room. My husband stayed with me until the team of doctors had to almost escort him out of the room. The doctors were all amazed as to how I had survived for so long without going completely paralyzed. The news had already spread around the hospital before I had arrived.

The questions were coming at me from all directions. Other doctors and nurses came in asking me how I survived. They wanted to know how I endured so much pain for more than three weeks.

My response was always the same, "By the grace of God." They were all calling me "the miracle woman" and were treating me like a celebrity. I was in too much pain to enjoy all the attention I was getting.

Finally, all of the doctors and nurses left my room for a while. I was told that many of them were interns and that they were anxious to talk with me some more. They introduced themselves and said that they were going to put some weights on me. That they were supposed to help ease some of my pain. But before this could happen, someone was going to take me to another part of the building for an MRI of the C-Spine. The procedure had to take place now at ten o'clock at night and I had to get out of bed. This sent me into a panic. They tried to calm me down by giving me some sleeping pills.

The pills took effect quickly because I was now calm and near to sleep before the test was over. The next thing I knew was, I was back in my bed and hooked up to the weights. What type of pills they gave me, I do not know. Nevertheless, it was very powerful and I needed some like them earlier at home.

The next thing I remembered was that at five the next morning, a nurse was waking me saying, "It is time for me to change your bed." I thought that this must be a crazy woman. How does she expect me to move strapped down with all of these weights on me? She must have read my mind because she said, "I am going to roll you back and forth from side to side."

Minutes later, a second nurse came in. She said that she was there to give me my bath. After she left, one more came in to feed me. I asked her why was I getting all of these good attention? She just said, "Because this is how we treat all of our patients, and you are a special patient." However, I loved every bit of it because those powerful pills had relieved some of my pain.

Later that morning, Dr. Noh came in with the papers for me to sign regarding my surgery. I was still frightened because he had already explained to me that it was a fifty-fifty chance that I might not survive the surgery. If I do survive the surgery, I might be paralyzed for the rest of my life. In addition, to make things worse, he said without the surgery I would die anyway, because no one can live with a broken neck. Since I had been in this condition for a few weeks, they did not know if I would make it through and there was no chance if I would ever walk again.

TERROR OF THE RED PANTS ATTACK ON DORCHESTER ROAD

I was so confused and frightened. I needed time to think without being under so much pressure. I needed time alone to pray and fast. This is what I had to do in order to set my mind at peace. I told the doctors that this was necessary before the surgery.

The doctors told me that I could not fast because I was on a lot of medication. That I could not stop my fluids, and that "the fast was out of the question." However, I explained to them that "God had kept me alive all of these weeks, and he was not going to allow me to die now." They tried to discourage me from fasting but my mind was made up. God would not have brought me to Dr. Noh just to allow me to die before he had performed the surgery on me. God is a God of second chances, and this was my second chance.

Therefore, that night I cried out to God, "Please, help me, Lord. Tell me what I should do." Later after I had prayed, I do not remember taking any medication. It was like I was in a trance. My eyes were closed but I was awake, and a voice said to me, "Do not be afraid, my child. You have nothing to worry about nor do you have anything to fear. I sent you here because Dr. Noh is the best in his field."

I was sure that this was God's voice speaking to me. I was no longer afraid, and it seemed as if my eyes just closed and I fell into a deep sleep. Early the next morning, I called for the nurse to come into my room. I told her to go tell my doctor that he could bring back the papers and that I was now ready to sign them.

The doctor came in. He asked me what made me change my mind overnight. He said, "I thought you said you needed two days to fast." I told him that I had a little talk with God and that he assured me that everything was all right. The doctor thought maybe I was a little off my rocker.

He said, "Oh." But the nurse just smiled and said, "Somebody helped her make up her mind." So, I signed the papers and the doctor told me that my parents had called and said they were on their way and that they would be arriving later that day.

I asked the nurse if she would dial my pastor's telephone number for me.

I wanted to inform him about the surgery the next morning. I called my husband to tell him that they had set a time for the surgery because it was in the critical stage and they could not delay it any longer. I asked one of the nurses if she would please call the newspapers for me because I had to tell my story just in case I did not make it through surgery.

The Interview with the Reporter

The reporter arrived within an hour. We talked for a few minutes. She asked me questions about the attack. We also talked about the Central Park attack on this young white woman. Three young black teens were accused of her rape and the beating that she suffered.

The reporter's name was Sheryl McCarthy. She was very sympathetic to my pain. It was a pleasure speaking with her. She took my story down and left the hospital promising that it would appear in the next day's paper. I disclosed as much as I could without impeding my pending lawsuit against the property owner. As promised, the next morning Sheryl had written a big write up about my attack.

People and cards started pouring in from all over the state. They had read my story in the newspaper. They wanted to see and hear from me. Flowers even came in from some woman in Albany, New York, who had read the story. She wanted to wish me well.

However, the lower courts said that the property owner was not at fault.

My lawyers went to Albany to the highest court, but the court would not hear their argument. Therefore, my lawyers informed me that they could not do anything else for me and that the case was closed. So, I can tell the entire story because the lawsuit is closed.

However, if the elevator had not been broken, there would not have been a need for me to be walking up eight flights of stairs. The lawyers did not file a suit against the doctors because they said that my injuries did not worsen because of the delay in my diagnosis. However, my condition did get worse but not by the legal terms of the law, they claimed.

However, knowing what I now know, I should have hired someone who specialized in accident cases only. Not realizing that my lawyers were experienced in criminal cases only, it was too late to re-open the case because two years had already passed.

Meanwhile, back at the hospital, my pastor came to pray with my family and me on the day of the surgery. After he finished praying, he said, "When I first walked into your room, it looked as if you had a halo over your head and a glow on your face." He said, "Not once, in all my years, had I ever seen one before." I explained to him about the talk I had with God the night before. Moreover, he said, "That explained the halo and the glow." He added, "I had lifted him up, when he had come to lift me up instead." He also said that he believed me and that glow were indeed signs from heaven. He left before I went into surgery but did not come back again.

I did not hear from him again until I returned to church more than a year later.

I was glad my parents made it to the hospital in time for my surgery. They were standing over me as the doctors were preparing to take me to surgery. We hugged and kissed. Both my parents had tears in their eyes. I knew that they were frightened in seeing their child lying there broken and bruised.

They knew that the only thing that they could do for me now was to pray. My father knew how to call up a prayer, and he prayed a prayer of faith. My husband came in minutes later, because he wanted my parents to spend some time alone with me first before the surgery. So, he joined in the prayer with us. After Pop had finished praying, the doctors came in and said, "It is time to go now."

My parents were tired after the long twenty-five-hour ride on the Greyhound bus, but they refused to go and take a nap. They were determined not to rest until my surgery was over. Therefore, they sat in my room until the doctor asked them if they could wait in the lounge area.

The Day of the Surgery

After my parents left my room, the doctor said it was time to prep me for the surgery. He said that in a few minutes, everything would seem a little fuzzy to me and that I should just relax and let the medicine take effect. He said that when I wake up, everything would be all over. He told me to close my eyes and that he was getting ready to stick a long needle in me.

I cannot remember when they rolled me down this long corridor to the operation room. They had already explained the procedures in advanced. How they would be doing two different surgeries on me at the same time? In addition, that the operation would be a long and risky one. They would have to remove some bone chips from the lilac crest area (that was from my left upper thigh and groin area). After that, they would place the bone chips into my neck to secure the bones back together.

They explained that although this type of surgery was risky, they had no choice because there was no way I could live in this present condition. The surgery lasted many hours. However, when I woke up in the step-down, I discovered that someone else was in my room with me. My mom was standing beside my bed, so I asked her to raise my head up a little.

When she raised my bed up, I saw that the person whom I was sharing my room with was a male patient. I became frightened at the fact that he was a man. I told my mom to let my bed back down quick and close the curtains. I rang for the nurse. When she came into my room, she asked me, "What seems to be the problem?" I said, "The problem is, there is a man in this room, and why am I sharing it with him?" The nurse said, "Look at him. He is paralyzed from the neck down. His operation was not as successful as yours was."

She said, "Now try to go back to sleep because you have not been out of surgery long enough to be awake." I felt sympathy for him and was relieved that he would not be walking in his sleep. Therefore, I asked my mom to raise the bed up again. I spoke to the young man and his eyes spoke back to me. My mom closed the curtains and put a clean gown on me.

The doctors had so many tubes in me: down my throat and in my vagina. I wondered why there was a tube in my vagina. Had they taken something out of it that they shouldn't have? One other thing that had me so puzzled was why they had to shave me down there also. Maybe they had taken my tubes out by mistake.

They even had these long rubber boots on both legs that went all the way up to my thighs. Therefore, instead of going to sleep as I had been told, I rang again for the nurse to come back. She explained that it was necessary that they shave my private area.

I went to sleep as directed. The next time I was awakened was when a doctor came into the room. He was sticking a needle in my arm and a sharp instrument up and down both legs while asking me if I feel anything. I said, "Ouch! That stings, Dr. Noh." He then called my husband and parents into the room. He informed them that I was going to be all right. However, by the look on the doctor's face, I knew there was something that he was not revealing to us. He kept asking me repeatedly how I felt.

This was my first time in the hospital having any type of surgery, and I had never had anesthesia before because before the attack, I had been a healthy forty-four-year old woman. Therefore, I kept telling the doctor that I was feeling good. What I did not know was that the anesthesia had not worn off as of yet. I said, "Thank God, and thank you Dr. Noh, for saving my life."

My husband and my parents had big smiles on their faces. However, two more doctors entered my room and they kept asking me the same question: "How do you feel?" I kept telling them that I was still in pain, but otherwise I was all right, I guess. When the anesthesia began to wear off, the tubes were still in my throat and what I thought was all right was not so.

I soon realized that there was something screwed into my head and on each side behind my ears. What looked like a halo was sitting on top of my head. The doctors explained that it was what they called the Philadelphia collar. It was to keep my neck in place and to keep me from trying to turn it.

They told me that they had also inserted some pins into my neck as well. They had explained most of the procedures to me before the surgery, but I had forgotten it. The doctors had also mentioned about drilling behind each ear a small hole to insert this piece of equipment.

They were not sure still if I would ever walk again or if my speech would ever improve. However, I was alive and not crazy and that was all that mattered. Four doctors had misdiagnosed my condition. Now I did not know who I was angry at the most: my attacker or the doctors who claimed that my shoulder was sprain and that I was sick in the head for questioning their diagnosis. They were trained doctors and I was only a patient. Nevertheless, I knew my own body—a body that God had given me.

Later that night when all of my visitors and my family had gone, I tried to fall asleep but I could not. All I could see was a pair of red pants and a pistol pointed in my face. I called for the nurse several times that night. Between the nightmares and the pain between my legs, I was a mess. I asked the nurse what was wrong with me. I was crying like a baby again. I thought after the surgery most of my pain would be gone. The nurse said that the doctor was still in the hospital and that she would beep him and have him come right away because she could not answer my questions.

This was a type of pain that I had not experienced before the surgery. The pain had moved from one part of my body to several other parts. The nurses came back several more times to try to quiet me down. They asked me why I was crying. I asked them if they were in pain and they said no. I said, "Well, my dear, then do not ask such a crazy question." So they increased my sleeping pills by giving me two different ones than the ones they had given me previously.

Finally, the doctor came in and explained that during the surgery they damaged another disc. He stated that it was unavoidable because they were trying to repair my broken neck. And that how the pins they put in to hold the fusion in place were causing me some discomfort also.

They did not tell me that in years to come, these same pins would eventually cause me all kinds of problems and how that skin would grow over them and no one would know that they were even there. This would cause pain to radiate from the neck all the way down the C-Spine.

The Two Miracles

After leaving the step-down, I woke up in a semi-private room. This time, I was sharing a room with a young lady who was in her twenties. Her head was completely covered in white gauze. She was crying out in pain. Such a cry I had never heard before. Although I was in pain myself, I stopped crying and asked the nurse what was wrong with this young lady. The nurses said that, "It was just a matter of time for her." That she had an inoperative brain tumor. The doctors had done all that they could do. They had already performed more than four surgeries, but the bleeding would not stop.

The nurses stated that she had recently gotten married but no husband showed up. The week I shared the room with her, the only visitors I witnessed were some church members. I tried very hard to comfort her because she was having a really bad time. However, there was not too much that I could do in my present condition, being in pain myself and still paralyzed on my left side.

Sometime later, two other female patients crossed my path. One of them had one leg cut off and the disease had spread. The doctors said that it was the only way to save her life. Later that day, a nurse said that they had to cut one of her toes off on her other foot.

The woman stated that she had inquired to the nurses about me, "the miracle woman." I wondered why she was asking the nurses about me. Why did she want to know about my condition? However, it was not about my condition the woman wanted to know. She had also heard that I was on the same floor as she was on. She had overheard the nurses and doctors discussing the miracle woman.

I asked her if she believed in God. She said, "Yes, I have faith in him." I then explained to her about the laying on of hands. Did she believe that the prayers of others could heal her if God so ordained? Her answer was, "Yes, I believe." Therefore, I laid my right hand on her legs and her feet because I still could not move the left. She thanked me and said, "I have confidence in your prayers." She said that she had heard about how I had talked to God. We talked a few more minutes and the nurse pushed me back to my room. Before I went to sleep that night, I whispered a prayer to God for the woman. I slept maybe two hours and was awakened by the nightmares. Waking up screaming, the nurses were around my bed trying to quiet me down.

Early the next morning, I had only gotten about two or three hours of sleep when a young girl entered my room. She said, "I am the daughter of the woman who you laid hands on her leg and toes yesterday." She added, "Thank you." And said that God had answered our prayers. She said that the doctor came in and said that they had made a mistake. That her mother's toe was just fine and she would be going home today. She hugged and kissed me, and we said, "Well by." This made me feel good because I knew God had heard and answered my prayer on behalf of the old woman.

Many other episodes took place concerning me and other patients. They had heard that the woman who had suffered a broken neck was indeed a miracle. That I was still alive after so many weeks. Many doctors came to see me. They all were speculating on how I survived in my condition for so long.

The nurse would tell me about the patients who were seriously ill. They would ask me to lay my hands on them. It was very late one night when a nurse came into my room. She said, "An old lady in her nineties has been sent here from the nursing home. She is in a coma and her son just wants to hear her voice one more time. The doctors have said there is no hope of her ever coming out of the coma." The nurses felt as if I had everything needed to heal everybody who needed healing. I was not God. I was just a broken woman who believed in God, and who just wanted to stop hurting myself. Therefore, this was one of my worse nights yet. The pain was so severe, the sleeping pills and pain medication did not work.

Looking up at the nurse and with tears in my eyes, I asked her, "What do you want me to do? Laying hands on people when I am just speaking incoherently myself? Someone had to take me to the bathroom and bathe me. However, you will have me steady going from room to room."

But the nurse said, "People have to see the miracle in you. They have to see how God saved you. You give them hope again. Just do not stop. They would say your speech might be just jitter for now, but people can understand. Your hands are what you use, so stop worrying about your speech. You have a gift that few have seen in the real world." I was not angry with them, I just wanted to stop hurting myself.

"I will get you out of bed, put you in a chair, and push you around to her room." I thought to myself, "This nurse is crazy." However, a soft voice said to me, "You are not here by accident. I kept you alive for this purpose. Just go. Whenever they ask you to go, just do not refuse them." Since I believed in the Holy Spirit, I knew it was God's voice speaking to me. Agreeing to go, the nurse pushed me around to this woman's room.

When we arrived in the old woman's room, all I could do was to sit and look at her. But, God said, "Lay your hands on her." She had a full head of the most beautiful white hair any person would love to have. Finally, I laid my hands on her forehead following his instructions. I then beckoned for the nurse to come and take me back to my room. After returning to my room, the nurse put me back into my bed, saying, "Good night, and thank you so much." That night, I slept good. Sleep came almost instantly. I had not slept like that since before the surgery when I had asked God about the operation.

Early the next morning, the nurse came running into my room. She was so excited and said that the old woman had awakened from her coma. She and her son were still talking as we speak. "He asked would it be all right to come and thank you?" the nurse said. I said, "Yes, let him come in." He came in and thanked me. He told me how long his mother had been in this coma and how the hospital had told him all about being a miracle women. All I could do was nod my head and touch his hand, then he left my room and I was never to see or hear from him again.

But word kept spreading throughout the hospital. Nurses and doctors visited me from other hospitals. Get well cards kept coming from many people I did not know. They had read the papers and heard about me. They wanted to make me something I was not. I was a broken vessel that needed repairing, and an angry person who questioned God as to why he would allow this to happen to me.

Nevertheless, always the same answer came back to me: "Who are you that I should die for you, and you not suffer any pain?" I thought then about Job, about how God had allowed Satan to test him, and how Job kept the faith. After weeks had gone by, the doctors felt I needed to start physical therapy and that I had to learn how to move my legs again. However, every time they would take me down to therapy, my legs would not move.

They did not know what to do with me, or at this stage, what to do for me. I tried telling them that they had done all that they were supposed to do for me. But they did not want to hear me. Every time they would take me down to therapy, the same thing would happen. The same thing was nothing. They would try to massage my legs before they took me down, but the legs would not move.

After I had spent weeks in the hospital, I saw no improvement. Therefore, I told the doctors to send me home. I felt that I would heal much better in my own familiar surroundings. Although they gave me many reasons why I should remain in the hospital, I was determined to go home. I felt, if my improvement was to come, it would come at home.

Coming Home from the Hospital

When the doctors saw that they could not convince me to stay, they discharged me and had me driven home in an ambulance. I had driven over the Brooklyn Bridge thousands of times in the past. However, this time was the longest ride I had ever taken over that bridge.

After finally reaching the apartment building, I said, "I am home at last." Entering the building, I noticed that the property owner had finally repaired the elevator. When I arrived on the eighth floor, my husband unlocked the door.

As the attendants wheeled me inside the apartment, nothing felt the same. Everything felt so strange to me. It was as if I was coming to a place for the first time. I had been gone for weeks and this did not give me a sense of belonging. Although I felt like a stranger, it was a good feeling to be back home again. The fear was still there, but I was at home. I could scream as loud as I wanted to and no one would be disturbed.

After the attendants had gone, I just wanted to sit there in my living room. I wanted to get a feeling that this was where I belonged. I wanted to stare at the furniture and at the pictures on the wall. I wanted to touch things because nothing in the apartment felt like it belonged to me. I felt like a stranger in someone else's apartment. I had lived in this same apartment more than twenty years. However, things just did not feel the same anymore.

If I was not already feeling terrible enough, to make things even worse, my husband said that he had to work that night and told me how he had promised his boss the day before. In addition, that he did not know that I was going to be coming home so soon. Had he known, he would not have volunteered to work. I was hurt and upset because I felt he could have called his job and explained his situation to them.

I felt that his job meant more to him than my health and safety. Therefore, I said to him, "Just put me to bed and go on where you are going." After putting me to bed and giving me two sleeping pills, he left. After tossing and turning for hours, I finally fell asleep. However, within a few short hours, I woke up screaming.

I dreamed that my attacker was coming through the bedroom window. I could not stop screaming. I was sweating and shaking all over. Finally, it was daybreak and I just laid there in a daze.

I was eager to come home despite knowing that my fears would be there. However, I had to come home because there was no place else to go. I wanted to be in my own private space. When I wanted to talk to God aloud, no one would look at me crazy. And no other patient would be disturbed.

I had some long conversations with God. Therefore, I screamed and cried, and yelled and screamed some more. Why did this have to happen to me? He had asked for my money and it was given to him. Why did he have to hurt me so bad? He had to be a professional robber. An inexperienced thief would have taken the jewelry and the money, and left.

I kept asking these questions to God. I needed some answers and God was whom I was confronting. I would talk to him because I knew he was listening. Therefore, I kept questioning him and saying to him, "Lord, this had to be an inside job. Someone had to have helped him. I was screaming, 'Please, do not kill me. Someone help me.' But no one came."

Many days, I cried and sobbed out loud while sitting there and not being able to walk and not do anything for myself. I felt helpless in being not able to use my left hand because it was still numb, as well as the big toe on my left foot. My speech had not improved and I could not move my left arm.

However, in my mind and spirit, I kept thanking God to be alive. In addition, as I kept reading Isaiah 40:28–31, these verses of scripture kept me strong and kept my mind in perfect peace.

TERROR OF THE RED PANTS ATTACK ON DORCHESTER ROAD

Especially verse 29 when He says, "He gives strength to the weary and increases the power of the weak." Had it not been for these few verses and my faith in God to heal, I really do not think I would have made it through my healing sane.

I really do think that I would have ended up in a mental hospital. There were many days when the pain was so severe and I had no one to talk with about the pain and the nightmares. I thought I would give up. However, I would read verse 29 over repeatedly. I was hurt and very lonesome. As I sit here now typing, my eyes are full of tears. These tears are because I am in a lot of pain to this day.

The doctors had already explained to me how long I would have to wear the neck brace. Moreover, for months to come, I would need assistance getting in and out of bed. I would also need assistance with needing and helping with my other personal needs. Therefore, the hospital ordered a home attendant and a nurse to care for me. As weeks and days went by, I longed for visitors from my church and my workplace.

But none came and the only visitors I saw every day were my housekeeper and the nurse. My housekeeper drank too much of the strong stuff. She worked only when she wanted to and spent long hours on the telephone. She dusted a few minutes and sat down. I had to let her go and asked for a new one. The new housekeeper was older and I had no problems with her. She and the nurse took good care of me.

On evenings when my husband came home from work, he would take charge as nurse and cook. Finally, one day Darlene called, she was a young new member in my church. She said, "I do not know how to pray, but I can come over and do some chores. Maybe bring some food, if you want me to." I was so happy. I said, "Yes, that would be good. I have a housekeeper and a nurse. They will let you into the apartment."

Darlene and her son Keith came that day and they came back several times. With every visit, she would always bring a dish or stop by the grocery and buy something tasty. They will always be very precious to me and remain in my heart forever.

The hurting part was that my pastor never called nor came to visit me. I was laid up for twelve months or longer. He would broadcast on his radio program every morning by calling my name; however, never once did he come to visit me. These were some difficult times for me because there were several ministers in my church under the pastor. However, none of them even came. On one Sunday after church, another member finally did come. She first went home and changed clothes.

She was an older female who wore a pair of short pants. I remember so well how she asked as she was leaving, "Could your husband go back downstairs with me?"

However, she had come up by herself. Women will try almost anything when they think they can flirt with your husband. He escorted her back downstairs as she had requested, but she never came back nor did she call.

Many of my co-workers were friends or so I thought. We had worked together nineteen years or more. Some of them started out in the company on the same day and some on the same year. Nevertheless, of all of my friends, only one of them came to visit me. That was my friend Juanita. She and I are still friends to this day. Although she had since married and moved to Jamaica, the West Indies, she still keeps in touch with me. We talk by telephone every few months. We send each other pictures and cards for almost every birthday and Mother's day.

There were a few co-workers who lived in my neighborhood but they did not come either. There were friends who lived in the building but they never visited either. They had come upstairs to my apartment many times over the years, but never came to visit during my confinement. I would see many of them outside the building on my going back and forth to doctors' appointments. They would speak casually and I would keep walking.

Finally, the time came for me to visit my company doctors again. They had made several threats that if I did not keep the next appointment, they would terminate me from the payroll and I would lose my entire pension, as well as my medical benefits. They had no compassion on their employees. Therefore, my husband took off work from his job so I could keep the appointment.

The job ordered the taxi service for me. That was their policy. When I entered the doctor's office, she said, "I did not know you were not able to walk without assistance of a walker."

I explained to the doctor that my doctors had sent all of my reports to the medical department. Moreover, I was certain that they all knew of my condition before I had arrived. The doctor spoke very cruelly to me, but I assured her that I was not in any mood to play these games with them. I told her, "Now get on with your examination. I need to go back home and lie down. I am in pain." The doctor then said, "I just need to ask you a few questions since you are still wearing that brace around your neck. I am afraid to examine you."

The doctor got me so heated but I kept my cool. I said, "These questions, I could have answered over the telephone. Why did you summon me to come here just to answer a few questions?" She then replied, "Well, that will be all for now. You are free to leave. The receptionist will call the car service to take you back home."

As the months went by, I had started to depend solely on my husband and housekeeper for all of my personal needs. I felt like it was time for me to take back charge of my life. Although I still could not move past the pain and the nightmares, I wanted to do for myself again.

I was tired of being a cripple because this was not who I was. I was a vibrant, outgoing person. Every morning, they would bring me into the living room and sit me in that same old chair with my Bible opened in my lap. I would read my scriptures first. Then I would try to get out of the chair falling with every try. However, I did not give up even when the nurse threatened to tie me to the chair.

I would then threaten to fire her if she did. Therefore, the nurse would keep quiet for a minute. Finally one day, I had enough of the housekeeper and the nurse trying to discourage me from trying to get up and walk. I knew that they meant well, but I had to try even if I failed in doing so. They were complaining about how my knees were scarred from the falling. They were really carpet burns because the floor had carpet on it. However, I was determined to try every day until I could stand on my own two feet again. I kept on trying. This went on for months, but I was sure of one thing and that was I had not lost my faith in God.

I was at a loss because I was a sports person who played on a softball team on Friday night mixed five bowling league. I was an avid bike rider and horseback rider in the park and I had walked in two marathons with my job. I worked as a volunteer on my off days for the American Red Cross, Blood Bank, and the Disabled Handicapped Children of the City of New York. Now to see myself depending on others for all of my personal needs was eating me up inside.

One day, I heard this soft voice again. However this time, the voice said, "It is time. Today is your day. Get up and move your legs." With my Bible lying across my lap, I stood up straight. The nurse and housekeeper yelled, "Please, we do not want to see you fall again today." However, I stayed standing and attempted to move my left leg. It moved. I then attempted to move the other leg and it moved. I started to cry. They ran over and bugged me.

Although I could not walk, nevertheless, the legs could move out from where I was sitting. The legs began to hurt, so I had to sit back down in the chair. A few minutes later, I tried to move again and this time they moved a little further. I was still in pain and could not walk. However, I could move and slide my legs a little. My legs were moving for the first time in almost a year. I was not sliding any more. I was walking.

I cried and sobbed aloud because I now felt a sense of completeness again. I knew without a doubt that I was on my way to being myself again. The nurse asked if she should call my husband and I said yes. When he entered the living room, I stood up in the chair. I began to move one leg forward after the other. I was able to move from the position that I was in. My husband fell down, hugged my legs, and said, "You never gave up. I now believe in God." That was the best news I had heard in years. He finally believed what I had been saying to him. Of all the years we had been married, I had never witnessed him cry. However, when he saw my legs moving, tears filled his eyes.

TERROR OF THE RED PANTS ATTACK ON DORCHESTER ROAD

I knew at that moment that it was time to start some real physical therapy. I needed more than just putting a hot towel on my neck and the tens on my legs. Although I had to get around with a walker, I was on my way back to the land of the living.

Moreover, I wanted to do my own bathing and all of those personal things for myself again. My desire was to take back control of my own life. The life that someone had stolen from me twelve months earlier.

My husband started to take me outside the apartment and down the block to try to strengthen my legs. Every day when he came home from work, he would do this. I could not walk any more than a block at first. However, the little walks did help me somewhat.

On my next follow-up visit with my doctors, they ordered me to see a speech therapist. He was one of the best therapists in all of New York City. Expensive but the best the state had. He was the famous therapist who worked with movie stars when they needed to learn how to speak English. He was good to work with and was very kind and considerate. After a year and a few months, he informed me that my speech was as good as it was going to get under the circumstances. Being that I was unconscious for a while, some of the cells that lead to the brain had died. Therefore, once they die, they do not regenerate.

Nonetheless, I accepted his diagnosis because the doctors had already told me from the beginning that I would never speak again. Therefore, if this is as good as it gets, then I was satisfied for now. However, I knew God and I knew he was able to do all things. What was impossible for man was not impossible for God. With my last visit at the speech therapist, I left his office expecting God to do the rest.

The pain was so intense until the medication just did not work and depression set in. I could not sleep and was like a zombie sliding out of bed and falling to the floor. I was stumbling around the apartment all night instead of in bed sleeping. I had to keep the walker away from the bed because I was afraid of falling over it. Therefore, I would leave it in the hallway, then try to crawl to it.

As the nightmares intensified, I knew that it was time for me to see another type of therapist. However, before I could make the appointment, my job called and said that I had to come again and visit their doctors. Upon my next visit to them, they were harassing me on a regular basis. When I entered the office, the doctor seemed to be more sympathetic this time. She explained that as she looked over all of my medical reports, that it would be beneficial to everyone concerned if I would consider going out on social security disability.

I looked at her, and said, "No, I am on sick leave and when I am able to return to work, I would." I explained to her that I had nineteen years invested in the company. Therefore, I was not leaving until I had twenty years of service. After twenty years, I could retire with benefits.

The doctor's whole expression now had changed. She then said to me, "The company does not want you back. You are a risk. You cannot even speak well any more. You can barely get a whole sentence out."

This was an insult to me. She had just tarred and feathered me in one sentence. She had worn me out with her words going back and forth. She really brought on an anxiety attack. My breathing got so heavy until my husband and I had to hurry out of her office. Outside on the streets, my husband hailed a taxi because a panic attack was on the way. My mouth got dry and my clothing was wet from my blouse down to my underwear. We had to call a psychiatrist soon as we arrived back home. The pain had also intensified, therefore my husband knew it was now bedtime.

My husband said that I just needed to lie down and relax for a while. This was a lot to digest in one meal. I felt as if I had gotten a piece of corn bread stuck in my windpipe. It was time to start thinking seriously about calling a lawyer. However, a voice said, "No, you know your condition. Your job cannot force you to leave. They are not supposed to discriminate against you when they know that you are out on sick leave."

That night, I had a horrible nightmare. It felt as if some people were watching me. I felt like they were looking through my bedroom windows. My husband had already closed the blinds, but I wanted the drapes closed, also. The nightmares were getting worse and more frequent now.

For months, the apartment was darkened. I was afraid that the man in the red pants was spying on me. Since I did not have to go out, I refused to let the light shine through. Fear had almost taken control of my life. Several months had passed and my neurologist advised me that it was time to talk to a psychiatrist. Fear was dominating my life, and there was no way I could ever heal with all of the fear. When we let fear control our lives, then we have no life at all. Our life no longer belongs to us. Fear is the dominant person. Although fear is not a person, it takes control over one's life.

Therefore, I shared his opinion. Dr. Friedman's, that is. It was time to seek the help from a psychiatrist. Something that I already known in my heart. I was just putting off the inevitable. The nightmares had worsened due to all of the stress from the company and their doctors. The sleeping pills no longer had any effect on me.

My husband and family members had no clue what was going on with me. Not all that I was going through, they could have not known. Although they sympathized with me, they really could not fathom the pain that was eating me up inside. My husband and I searched through the yellow pages and found a therapist who was willing to see me in a couple of days.

Upon arriving at her office, we realized that we had to walk up six flights to her apartment. However, after that initial visit, I knew there was no way that I would not be going back to see to see her again. The idea of being in a strange building with a sixth-floor walk-up sent chills through me. It was after we had arrived at the door of her office that we discovered she was using her apartment as an office

She made us feel welcome. However, she asked my husband if he would remain in another room. The room he waited in was her kitchen. When the therapist and I began to talk, she immediately asked about the attack. I went into another panic attack, as I began to sob. The therapist said, "Let us change the subject."

Instead, she questioned me about my marriage. She said she understood and that it was just too painful to talk about at that time.

She then went to explain to me that how she also had been a victim of a crime. Explaining how after months of feeling sorry for herself, she went back to school, got her license, and became a therapist. Her goal was to help other victims of crimes.

She also explained that she was only a therapist and that she could not prescribe any medication for me. However, she knew of a very good psychiatrist who she often recommended some of her patients to. She would call him later and have him give me a call. I thanked her, and my husband and I left her apartment.

After arriving back home, I was exhausted, so my husband helped me into bed. It was no longer than one hour after I had gotten into bed when the telephone rang. The man said, "My name is Dr. Stuart Kleinman." He added that Dr. Hellenbach had given him a brief description of my condition, and that he worked strictly with victims of crimes only and that he would be glad to take me on as one of his patients.

He set up an appointment for two days later. From the first visit, we discussed everything not related to the attack. After the third session, we talked a little but he was gentle with me in easing into the subject. He did not pressure me. He allowed me to talk at my own pace. On my fifth visit, he taught me how not to blame myself anymore for the attack.

Several times, he tried to put me under hypnosis, but it failed every time. He just could not get me to go to sleep. Maybe it could have been out of fear, I do not know. He explained that hypnotherapy had helped many of his patients. However, after about the fourth time, he never tried anymore.

Dr. Kleinman noticed that every time I had a session, the anger and bitterness swelled up in me. I tried to explain to him that I was also angry with myself because I should have tried to fight back. How could I just stand there and allow this man to beat me the way that he had? I never attempted to fight back. Was I a coward?

Since this was my fourth visit, I thought that I would feel some relief. However, the doctor explained to me that this was a long process and how he would prescribe me some new medication. This new medication would help ease some of my anxiety. He prescribed an anti-depressant to help with the Prozac that he had already prescribed.

I explained to the doctor how that it would be hard for me to give to people begging again on the streets again after my attack. That I had always been a charitable, trusting, and loving person. If ever anybody needed anything, I would give freely without asking any questions. Homeless people on the streets, I would give them because I knew they needed it. If my attacker had only asked me, I would have given him my last. But he hurt me and took something away from me. How can I move on?

After his office visit, I was scheduled for physical therapy. Upon arriving, I expressed that it was for them to do more than just put a hot towel and tens on me. However, they said, "You are still wearing that full collar and we cannot take the risk of a lawsuit."

My visits cost my insurance $200.00 per hour and not a second longer. However, they did write me a prescription for my own tens unit to use at home. Physical therapy was tiring that day because of the hour I had spent at Dr. Kleinman's office.

Arriving back home from therapy, I was exhausted again. Therefore, my husband bathed me and put into bed. I was too exhausted to eat that day. Although my legs were moving, I still could not take care of all of my needs by myself.

At times when the pain seem to be unbearable and non-stop, those crazy thoughts would try to creep back into my mind. But that small voice would be there saying, "Your life was saved for a purpose. And do not even think what you are thinking." I would pick up my Bible and start to read my favorite scripture. By the time I finished reading, those crazy thoughts would be gone.

Not counting the two pills that Dr. Friedman had me on, Dr Kleinman had me on four different pills: one for anxiety, another for sleeping, another one for depression, and Prozac. I thought to myself that I had to find a way to take control and get off some of those pills. I just did not want to become a legal addict.

I constantly prayed for God to give me the strength to get off the pills, and for the nightmares and the pain to stop.

On my next visit to Dr. Freidman, he read the latest CAT scan that he had ordered. He explained that he had some good news and some bad news to tell me. He asked which one he should tell me first. "Let me hear the good news first," I said. He said that eventually my pain would get better, but my condition would get worse as the years went by. This was a hard statement for me to grasp. How could my pain get better but the condition worsen over time? He explained how my spine would deteriorate because of the type of surgery they had performed on me.

With a compressed spine, deterioration of the upper spine would move down the spine, that there was nothing anyone could do to repair it, that eventually in years to come I would not be able to move at all, and how I would never be the same person that I once was and that this would all take place in about ten years.

I became angry with him, angry because I did not want to hear any negative talk about becoming fully paralyzed in ten years. I was somewhat happy to be able to move slowly around now. "Let the years take care of itself. Please, do not spoil this today," I said. He reminded me of how my speech was almost incoherent. Moreover, that I would not be able to lift anything over ten pounds again. I would never be able to go bowling again. There would be no more bike riding for me, either. I could walk, but limit the running to five minutes at a time. I had limited use in the turning of my head and I won't be able to look up at the sky again.

When I left his office, I had made up my mind that I was never going back for another visit. However, I did go back because he was my neurologist. He was kind and honest, and his patients always came first. He would often tell me that I was his miracle patient.

Weeks passed and one day my job called and said that they had made several appointments for me. They said that they would be sending me to see several specialists. I went to every appointment that they had made. However, after visiting each of them, they came back with the same reports as my own doctors had already reported to them. They were trying to get their group of specialists to dispute my own private doctors' reports as if they were lying.

TERROR OF THE RED PANTS ATTACK ON DORCHESTER ROAD

Dr. Friedman had already stated to them that he felt like I needed to be around people again. Just sitting at home in my apartment was doing more harm than good. He would send me back to work with limited hours and restricted duties. My psychiatrist agreed with him that it was necessary that I did return to work and that I needed to be around familiar faces again.

After the company had received all of my doctor's reports, they started making doctors' appointments for me in every direction again. They had me traveling from one point to the other despite knowing that I was not able to do all of that traveling. I knew that they were trying to discourage me from returning to work, and they wanted these doctors to agree with them.

They threatened me that if I did not return to work that they would fire me now that they were harassing me not to come back to work. Therefore, I had to let them know that, since they had been harassing me to return, they had to find work for me to do. It could be in another job description but the pay had to be the same as it was before I went out sick.

Therefore, I knew the rules because I had been the union representative a few years earlier. So, I knew what they could and could not do to me. I was so good as the union person until they found a way to take me down. They made an offer to be a supervisor. They knew that I always wanted to be a supervisor, so I took the supervisory position. Therefore, I had to give up the union position because I could not represent the people and suspend them, too. This was part of their strategy and I fell for it. But the position did not last for long. I had to give it up. I just could not do the things to people that the other supervisors were doing.

Therefore, the job kept saying that I must go out on Social Security Disability. I argued back that, no, the company has an obligation to find work for me to do. There were several more weeks of confrontation between the company's medical department and myself. The last one was a bitter one because I was going to return to work. Since nothing they would say to me would make me change my mind, the words got ugly.

When a person presumes to be a physician, they are expected to have morals. But this particular person talked to me like a street person would. The hell they put me through was something I would not wish on anyone. I just was not used to being treated so mean and nastily. Professional people usually hide their words and thoughts, but not the ones I was dealing with. Never a caring word like, "I am sorry you were attacked and beaten." "How do you feel now?" "What can we do to make your life a little easier?"

I just find it so hard to believe even today as I sit here and write. All of the pain and the hurt feelings come back as if it were yesterday. I pray always that I will never have the heart to say and do those types of mean words to another person.

When I have gone on interviews, people ask the question: How do you get along with others? How do you treat your fellowman? I am sure these people were asked those same questions, so they must have lied on their applications.

My Return to Work

I finally returned to work after a year out on sick leave. I was to work four hours a day. My hours would be 8:00 a.m. to 12:00 p.m.. I would have one hour on, and fifteen minutes off. My off days would be Monday through Friday. There would be no weekends or holidays. I would be on light duty and no lifting anything no more than five pounds. I was to do no bending, no reaching, and no climbing. These were my restrictions from my medical doctors.

But that first day was like hell. They treated me as if I had leprosy. The managers spoke to me as if I were a new employee, especially Mrs. Wainwright. She said, "You should have just stayed home. You will never be able to do any meaningful work here again." I never knew people could be so cruel to one another, especially the people that supervised. I have seen people with communicable diseases treated with more kindness that I was being treated.

I remember when this manager was hired. She had just come over from the West Indies, and none of the other managers cared for her. Knowing that she was new and needed a friend, I treated her as if she had been with the company for years and treated her like a sister. Now since she had become a manager, she was telling me that they had no place there for me any longer.

That very moment, I felt that someone had put a knife in my back. The thought of a woman who I befriended speaking down to me in that manner was reprehensible. Especially when I was the one who helped her out with lunch money. She had finally made manager and now she was stepping on everyone under her. She spoke as if she were God himself. I was deeply hurt. I tried to fight back the tears. However, I could not. The tears kept coming. They would not stop, so I hurried into the women's room and almost dropped my walker.

While in the women's room, all I could think about was that I had more years in seniority than this manager had and she was speaking to me as if I was a newly-hired employee. I dried my tears and walked back into the office. Mrs. Wainwright said, "Sit here at this desk for your four hours, because I have nothing for you to do. You can just leave when it is time for you to go."

I had given this company nineteen years of my life. The company had honored me for perfect attendance for many of those years. I was always coming in early before anyone else arrived, because I did not like rushing. I wanted to have time to relax before starting to work. Many times I came into work sick because they were short of people, and I wanted to help out wherever I could.

When there was snow on the ground, I would walk five miles with snow up to my waist. There were times when the subway and buses did not operate because of the snow. I would stay overnight sleeping on carts that the company had set up for their employees.

Many employees could not come into work because they were on the bus or the subway lines, so when the company needed volunteers, I would always say yes. Oftentimes on these sleepovers, we would sleep for two hours and work three alternating between the volunteers. When there was not enough people to work the telephones, we had to work sixteen hours with no sleep.

Working many holidays and giving up my off days just to help the company out was commonplace. I loved my job and did not want to lose it. I enjoyed being a dependable and on-time worker. But now, none of that mattered to them because they were treating me as if I was a stranger, and I was not going to allow them to do that. Therefore, I made it plain to them that I will continue to come back every day until they find work for me. That I will not let them force me out without a fight.

The same supervisor who was trying to discourage me had undergone a very serious operation on her back at one point. She was out of work almost a year herself, and no one tried to discourage her from returning to her livelihood. She was also on restricted duty and not able to perform her regular job. However, she had people who were under her, so she pushed her work off on them. This cut me deep into my heart because I had taken her under my wings.

When others laughed at her behind her back about the cheap homemade clothes and cheap shoes she wore, I would always make excuses for her, saying maybe that is all she could afford at this time, and reminded them that many of us started out that same way. We did not always have fancy clothes, either. But as time went by, we started to dress in fashionable clothing. Therefore, we should never make fun of another person's wardrobe because we never know where we will end up.

I remember one day asking this supervisor, "Did all my loyal years not account for anything?" She did not answer me. All she said was, "Just go and sit in the conference room. Make sure you close the door behind you. When it is time for you to go home, just get up and leave."

The conference room had one window that faced the bus stop. There was nothing in the room except one long table and chairs. There was nothing to do but look out the window. There was no one to communicate with, and being isolated in this room and looking out the window had totally shut me off from everyone.

They humiliated me. I did not deserve to be treated like this. Even slaves got a chance to mingle and talk to each other. The tears ran down my cheeks, but this was not going to deter me. I kept pleading with them to give me my nineteen years' pension and I would gladly retire. However, every time I asked, they would say no. I would respond back with, "Then look to see me every day for four hours for the next five years. I will retire then and only then, and no one can stop me."

On occasion, a few older employees who started out with me would come into the room and talk. They were not afraid of the supervisors because there was nothing that they could do to them. Sometimes when a manager saw them, they would chase them out of the room. However, they would always return later to chat.

One day after work, I received a telephone call shortly after arriving home. The person on the other end said, "You need to call the union because they are treating you unfair, and some of us do not appreciate it at all. Just like they are mistreating you, one day one of us might fall into that same situation as you are now in. Do not take this type of unfair treatment any longer. We are not used to seeing you so passive because you have always been so outspoken. Now you are letting them push you around and you are not fighting back. You fought for us as our union representative and even carried the company to court. The person we see every day is not you. Girl, fight back."

The telephone call put some extra fight in me. So, I called the union and explained the situation to them. The representative said, "Tomorrow, go back into the conference room. Do not argue with them because someone from the union will be there. We have to be an eyewitness of you in that room with the doors closed."

So the next morning, I went back to my seat in the conference room and closed the door. About a half hour later, the union person walked into the room. She said, "I will now go and bring your manager in here. I need her to explain to me why she has you closed off from other people. You should be out in the open doing something instead of just sitting here. I am sure they have some paper work for you since they claim they are always behind."

Seconds later, the union person came back in with the supervisor. She opened up the union rulebook and began to read the bylaws. She then explained to the supervisor that she did not want to see this type of abuse again in any of their offices. She said, "You cannot lock her away for four hours a day. Even prisoners get a chance to communicate with other prisoners. This type of abuse only adds to her depression and you are in violation. You have just broken many of the union contract rules. I will be in touch with your manager this day. Have you forgotten that this is a communications company? We do not treat our employees in a manner like this. Would you want someone to treat you like this?"

The union person came back and spoke to me again in private. She informed me that if I had any more problems to not fail to call them. She said that I have a right to communicate with my fellow employees and the company cannot stop that.

TERROR OF THE RED PANTS ATTACK ON DORCHESTER ROAD

After the union person left, the manager told me to come and sit at the desk next to hers. Minutes later, she came and dumped a pile of papers on the desk. She did not say a word she just walked away. Therefore, I did not ask any questions either, I just got up and went on my break. After returning, someone had left a note on top of the pile of papers. The note read, "this is the old clerk's desk." I already knew who desk it was so why was she telling this to me, I wondered. The note also read, "you will run errands for me and the other managers."

I only wished I had kept that note, for it would have been nice to put in this book.

I remember one day she sent me to the pharmacy to buy her some sanitary napkins. She said, "make sure you stop by the other managers' desks to see if they need anything from the outside." Some managers asked me to bring them lunch back. While others smiled and said maybe, tomorrow when you run errands for her you can run for us also.

Weeks had gone by and they were paying me my regular salary. Therefore, I was not losing anything by running errands for them. The walking was not good for my legs because of the pain but I did it anyway. If the company wanted to pay me my salary to run errands, so be it.

Therefore, I decided to count it all joy because since they had me running errands for them, I might as well do my own little shopping and pay my bills while I was out on company time. The managers joked about it to my face. They hurt me more than anyone will ever know.

The laughing and the snobby remarks. They would say things like, we have a list of supplies for you to buy today. None of them even, asked how my pain was. I was still wearing the collar and walking with a cane they did not care.

They laughed at me as if I was nothing but a joke. I just did not care, I thought in my mind. But of course I cared because I had feelings too. So let them laugh, I was paying my bills, and was getting my regular paycheck, so you tell me who was laughing the loudest.

They thought that I would get tired of the humiliation, and figured that if they disgraced me enough I would just go out on Social Security, and forget about my years of service. They had made up their minds they were not going to offer me disability. Therefore, I had made up my mind also, I was not going to give them the satisfaction of leaving; I was in it for the long haul. Many times, I asked them for work. However, every time the supervisor would say the same thing, we have nothing for you to do here.

On one occasion, Mrs. Wainwright informed me that she was leaving. She stated that the company had decided to transfer her to another office. The question in my mind was, why she felt as if she had to inform me. It mattered little to me if she went or stayed. Maybe she just wanted to see what my response would be. I think of no other reason why she felt as if she needed to inform me.

Later on that same week, some of my co-workers came around with a list. These particular ones were the people who had not spoken to me since my return back to work. These were the managers' pets, their snitches. I knew they wanted me to say something nasty. So that they could go back and report it to her.

They said, "we are giving the manager who is leaving a party. Would you like to contribute to the list?" I politely said, "no thank you, count me out."

A few days had passed before the new manager would arrive. Finally, on a Monday morning, she walked over to me. She introduced herself as Mrs. Kallester. She said, "I am your new manager." She spoke very politely and asked me how I was feeling. She said that the other managers had told her about my condition. They also told her how I was not able to do any meaningful work.

However, in my experience, she said I feel like they were mistaken. She went to say that she knew that I was able to do much more than they said that I could Saying that, she said that she was going to give me a test to see exactly what I did qualify for. In addition, if I pass the test, they would transfer me to another location.

I was shocked because I realized that she had not read my medical reports and my restrictions. If she had, she would have known that I could not travel in my condition. The doctors had me classified as being health-impaired, which meant that they would have to place me in a position equal in pay and no traveling. The work would have to be within walking distance.

I had overheard some employees saying that this new manager had not earned her title as of yet. They had sent her to this office to prove herself and then receive her title. Well, I was not about to let her make me her scapegoat. So I calmly and politely asked if she had read my medical reports herself and my restrictions?

Her answer was, "No, I have not. But your previous manager briefly explained your situation to me." I informed her that I did not have to take a test nor did I have to travel to another borough. She then said that she would have to read my reports for herself and speak to me again in a day or two.

I had to call the union again and complain about what was now going on. How this new manager wanted to send me, on the subway to another location. Upon arriving the next day, the manager asked me to follow her into her office. She started to say that she had read my file overnight and that she was sorry.

"Could you forgive me for not taking the time to read it for myself," she asked? I accepted her apology with a smile but knew from the look on her face she was planning yet something else. Therefore, I was preparing myself for what ever she had in mind next.

A few weeks went by and Mrs. Kallister told me that she was going to loan me to another department. That the place is going to be close in distance where I was now at. That it would be in walking distance just ten minutes away.

She told me what my duties would include. Some light filing, some standing, computer work, loaning out books, and tapes. That this would be a Librarian assistant. The Librarian was going on leave to have her baby. Therefore, she had to train someone to take her place before she left.

Therefore, they sent me over to the company's Library. The walk was a short distance about four blocks away from the office where I was. This was a temporary assignment but I was happier than I had been in months.

There would be no manager over me anymore just a Librarian. I would be working with her for a few months. After that, I would be on my own until she returned from having her baby. All of this seemed like a good deal to me, I was not complaining.

Upon arriving at the library, a young woman introduced herself as Marbara. She said that she was attending college part time, working on her second master's degree. That she was not an employee of the company. That she worked as a private contractor.

She explained how she would train me in all the aspects of the job. That she wanted me to learn everything that goes along with the job of a Librarian. There would be times when she would have to leave for her early classes or her late classes, and that I would be by myself in the Library.

Therefore, it was best if I learn everything that I could. That sounded very good to me because training for a Librarian would be a feather in my cap. I was very excited because I was on my own and learning a new position. Since I already knew the computers because that is what I had been working on for eighteen years already.

All I had to do was to learn the logon procedure for the library. That turned out to be very easy. Two weeks had gone by and Marbara had taught me all that I needed to learn. The fact was I could manage the library as good as she could. She said that I was a quick learner because in a couple of weeks I had learned all the functions of the job. She said that she was more than pleased with her quick study. Normally it would take someone a month or two to teach all of the procedures, especially the billing part. But she was more than happy with me.

The next morning Marbara called to say that she would be in late or she might take the entire day. She said that she had to study for a couple of tests before she went to school that night. She told me that I would be on my own, but I should have no problems.

That next day several managers came in to check out books and tapes. Several managers made comments on how they found what they needed within a short period. That day went very well and I was pleased that no one made any complaints. The managers all smiled and they thanked me for doing a good job.

When it was time for school break, Marbara took a week off for vacation. During that week, I had the entire library by myself. Again, things went very smooth; there were no complaints. Every customer was satisfied, some even brought me coffee, which I did not drink. I have never been a coffee drinker and to this day still do not drink it.

Marbara had done a good job; she had trained her assistant well. She knew her assistant was no threat to her because she was the Librarian. She had her masters and was working on her second one in communications. Therefore, she was not worried with or intimidated by my help.

Although, I do not believe that her manager was so thrilled at how Marbara had trained me so well in such a short time… She was upset that she had taught me so much. She and her manager, were close friends. They lived in the same neighborhood and she had gotten Marbara that position.

One-day Marbara's manager came into the library, Marbara had just returned from vacation. She and her manager were in a corner speaking in a very low voice. I was busy at the computer checking in some books. Therefore, I could not hear what they were whispering about. However, it was an intense conversation because several times they raised their voices.

Finally, her manager left and she came over to me and said. I am sorry to tell you but you will no longer work on the computer. Instead, you will be filing and unpacking the new books and tapes as they arrive. You will also be responsible for unpacking the old periodicals in order of year and date. Why are all these changes so sudden I asked? She just responded by saying, "this is the way my boss wants it."

I had to remind her that I could not do any bending or reaching over my head. Explaining that I would not be able to lift any heavy books over five pounds. I explained that they would have to get someone to come in and put the boxes on the table in order for me to pack them away.

She said, well since you cannot bend or lift you can just file the books that are on the return label. Her whole approach changed after she and her manager had their little talk. Whatever her manager had said to her she had changed toward me; she were not so friendly anymore.

Her manager worked for the company; therefore, she probably had spoken to my manager, they did not want me to succeed in the library because they wanted me out of the company. They knew Marbara was expecting a baby soon. I think they were afraid she would leave me in charge.

I thought that was the reason why they had sent me there in the first place. It was because she would be going on maternity leave. Otherwise, why would they send me there unless they were convinced that I would not be able to learn and would surely leave the company. Whatever was going on, changes were about to be made and in my gut I knew it.

The next day Marbara was absent but her manager, Mrs. Pickwick was waiting for me. She told me that Marbara had said that I was not happy working there in the library. I told her that I had never said that and why was she trying to start confusion between Marbara and myself? She said if you are not happy here, I could send you back to your office.

I asked her why was she being so mean and rude to me, that I had no complaints. I told her that I did not want to go back to my office. She already knew that I did not want to complain. Although I was well aware that this was what she wanted me to do. What they were asking me to do would cause me more pain and harm.

Therefore, if I wanted to remain there I would have to bend down and unpack those boxes. From her tone of speaking, I knew they were not going to have anyone come in and lift those boxes for me. They had me caught in a difficult situation. With me trying to weigh it all was a bit much for me right then.

I felt anything would be better than going back to my old office. Mrs. Pickwick knew that she had me up against a wall as she thought. I now realized that was the biggest mistake I had made. My agreeing to do anything just to make myself useful. That was the wrong thing to do in my condition. My doctors had ordered me not to do certain things and now I had agreed to do them. I was just trying to stay on the job for four more years until I reached my twenty-five years.

Weeks went by, I started to feel more pain in my neck it was intensifying. The medication was not helping with all of the straining and bending. I was afraid to complain, therefore, I decided to double up on my medication hoping it might give me some comfort. I also had to double up on my depression medication, thinking that if I stayed drugged up, I would not hurt so much.

However, there were days when I had to triple all doses of medication. The boxes were extremely heavy and that made the pain worse. One day, I could not get out of bed, so I called the office to inform them what was going on and told them that I was in a lot of pain because I was doing things that my doctors had restricted me from doing.

A manager told me that Mrs. Kallester had left and went back to her old office. There was a new manager from upstairs who had come down to take her place. They gave me another telephone number to call. When I dialed the number, the voice on the other end said, "Hello, this is Mrs. Pumeria."

I tried explaining to her who I was, the trouble I was having in the library, and how they were ignoring my restrictions, which called for certain things I was not supposed to do. However, for weeks they had me doing them. I did not want to be a constant complainer so I kept quiet. At this point, I can no longer keep quiet because it is causing me more harm.

Mrs. Pumeria advised me that I should not complain so much. That I should be glad that I had a job. "What is a little pain?" she said, and that there was nothing for me to do back in my old office. She did not give me a chance to say anything more because she cut me off by saying "well, bye" and hung up.

I really did not want to keep calling the union, but I had no choice. Therefore, I called and spoke to Mrs. Mavastimox who said that she did not want to deal with this manager. She said that she had dealt with her in the past and she was not easy to talk with. She went on to say that they would not find anything for me to do. I thanked her and hung up. "I then told Marbara, my supervisor, that I was in severe pain and was going home sick."

I took a taxi and went directly to Dr. Friedman's office. I informed him of the situation and all the pain I was suffering and how I had almost tripled all of my medication. He was very concerned about my condition and about the tripling of the medication. He said that he knew I would not be able to do much work, but I needed to be doing something.

But since the job insisted that I returned or be let go, he put me on restricted duties. He said he would put me on a stronger pain pill. Therefore, I should remain in bed a couple of weeks until the pain had left.

So, I took his advice and called my job. I told them what my doctor had advised me to do and that he had put me on bed rest for two weeks. However, when I returned, I would not be going back to the library. I would be coming back to my old office and we would talk then.

But after the two weeks were up, I went back to my old office. However, when I arrived, they said that I had to return to the library. So, I went back and upon arriving, they told me to go across the street and work and that the library was moving over there. They wanted me to set things up over there at the new location. My duties had changed. They now consist of separating books, putting them in order, etc.

I knew something did not sound correct, but I went along with the program. I wanted to see what the outcome would be.

The manager told me that the employees across the street do not start work until eight-thirty. Therefore, since my hours were eight until four, I would have to wait in the lounge until eight-thirty or else I could change my hours to match there's.

I had to remind her that my hours could not be changed. That these were restricted hours that the company's medical department had set up for me. They set these hours up so that I would not get caught up in the rush hour traffic. I just could not change them even if I wanted to, but I did not want to.

I asked her why they would not give me a key to let myself in. I had a key before I came across the street. So why can't I have a key now? The manager said that maybe she would see about me getting a key. Therefore, the next day I walked over to the library. Shortly after I arrived, Marbara called. She said that I had to come back across the street to the main library for a while longer.

As I was filling, I came across a memo that read "I am sorry to inform you, Mrs. Pickwick, but we cannot release Memsey from her position here at the moment. We will allow her to come to the main library next Monday." That is why they were sending me across the street and I knew that it had nothing to do with setting up the new library.

She did not want me on the computer any longer. The office that Memsey worked in was closing due to job cutbacks. It is my belief that Mrs. Pickwick was doing Memsey's manager a favor. Managers often did favors for each other.

Mrs. Pickwick and Marbara were not woman enough to tell me the truth. They felt as if they did not owe me any explanation, so they did not give one. Friday before I left for home, Mrs. Pickwick told me to report on Monday back across the street.

Monday morning, I reported as told but no one came to let me in. About eight fortyfive, a young woman finally arrived. She apologized for being late. I told her that it was very cold out there in the lounge. She said, "It is very cold in the library as well." She smiled and said that they have to work in their coats and jackets year-round over here.

My pain is always worse when I get cold. It has been this way since the surgery. My bones ache. They were giving me more chores to do that were on my restriction list of not to do. I was aware of what they were trying to do. They were trying to push me to the limit.

Therefore, I tried very hard not to get into a confrontation because I knew what their game was. I needed to stay on the job. I now needed about three more years to go. Nothing or no one was going to make me lose that seniority. One thing I knew for sure: I was not going anywhere until my service pension was bridged.

They wanted to make me angry so that I would walk away. However, I was too stubborn to allow them the opportunity of doing that. I had too much to lose.

Bridging my service would not happen if I left. I was not going to lose all those years in the company. Yet, the harder they tried to push me out, the more determined I was to stay.

In 1983, the Federal Government said that the company was too large. As a result, it was broken up into small companies. They said that the company was monopolizing all the small businesses. That was cause for the break up in the company.

Because of the breakup, the company started downsizing. Many of us were forced to go to one of the other communications companies. When the company did not get enough volunteers, they forced people to go who had less than twenty years in seniority. I was one of the ones who was sent to the other company.

We had plenty of work to do in the beginning. We were able to recoup the company millions of dollars in back payment. However, when our assignments were over, the company claimed that they did not need all of us. So, they laid us off after two years. Therefore in 1985, we were without a job.

Our primary company did not take us all back. We had to be rehired because their excuse was that they had a surplus and that they no longer needed us, so we were out of a job. We were more than just out of a job, we had to fight to get back into our original company. They made us all take the tests over again as if we were new employees.

When we re-applied, we lost two years of service pension. We also had to be back at the old company for five years before they would bridge our service back. Since I had not yet reached my five years back when my attack took place, I had to hang in there at all cost. Whatever it took, I was not going to let them drive me out without a fight.

The managers did not understand nor did they care because they brought all of the old managers back. They did not lose any of their service time. Every day, Mrs. Pickwick would give me something to do that I just could not physically do. They did not care that my neck was still in a collar and that I had to walk with a cane.

One day, there were many boxes on the floor filled to capacity with old books. They were in my path. I tried to get around them, but ended up falling over them and hurting both arms and legs. I had bruises all over my knees and legs. I said enough is enough. I am not going to allow them to treat me like this any longer. I am not a new employee with no rights. I have rights.

I picked up the phone, dialed my old office, and demanded that I speak to Mrs. Pumeria. When she answered, she sounded polite until she heard my voice. Her voice then changed immediately. "What do you want now?" she asked. I explained to her that I was in severe pain because I had fallen over some boxes and had bruises on both legs and arms.

In addition, that it was extremely cold there in that new office. They told me that they could not adjust the temperature for my benefit only just because I was in pain. I explained to her that I could not continue bending down as I had been doing of unpacking boxes and falling all over the place. She repeated herself, "You should be glad that you have a job to fall on."

I thanked her for listening, hung up, and called the union. This time, I had taped our conversation. Therefore, when the union person came on the line, I tried explaining to her about the inhumane treatment I was getting and that I knew that the company could find something better for me to do.

The union person told me that I should stay where I was at. She said, because in my condition, there was not anything they could do for me. I said, "No, I am not going to stay here. Why am I paying you'll thirteen dollars a week for dues? I needed help and I need it now." I was not going to spend another day in that library. I would sue the union and the company. And as soon as I hung up from her, I was leaving the library.

I told her that as soon as we finish this conversation, I will be leaving the library. If necessary, I will sue the company and the union because I am tired and I was not going to take any more of this abuse.

So, I left the library and informed the manager in charge that I was going back to my office. I knew this was a bold move, but I was at a point where I was not going to sit there in pain, in the cold with a jacket on, and doing chores that I knew would cause me more damage.

I figured that if they wanted to fire me, let them. Then I would have a good court case against them. I went home and made several phone calls to different organizations. I explained my situation to each of them. They in turn explained my rights under the disability act of New York State. They explained my rights were indeed being violated and that my union knew it, also.

This calmed me down a lot. Early the next morning, I went down to my old job and requested that I speak to the supervisor in charge. ·They told me to take a seat in her office, and when she had a chance, she would speak to me. About an hour later, she came in and I told her that I knew my rights, of how I had spoken with the State Disability Board, and that they informed me that they were violating my rights.

" I said, "Therefore, I am back in this office to stay and I am sure that you can find suitable work for me to do. I am tired of the way you have belittled and humiliated me. I am a person and I have feelings, too. In addition, I am tired of you trying to force me out on Social Security Disability. I am not going anywhere until you bridge my service dates. Now, if you want to fire me, go right ahead and do so because I have a tape message of our last conversation. The manager looked at me as if she wanted to curse. However, all she said was, "I should write you up for insubordination." I looked into my purse, took out my pen, and said, "Start writing because I am here to stay."

The managers loved to threaten you, but at this point, I was hurt beyond repair. So, what else could they do to me? She then looked at me, and said, "Girl, calm yourself down." She put on a silly smile, because she knew they had not broken me and I was there to stay.

She told me that she would have someone to train me, and that after my training, I would become one of the office's payroll clerk. She added thay they were in need of a grade three clerk to work from that office and that our payroll clerks were in the Manhattan and Queens office. Moreover, my training would take place there in that office. They knew that I could not travel to Manhattan to the training school. Due to the fact that I was classified as health impaired, the instructor would be coming to me.

Therefore, she would be sending the other acting clerk, whom they had been using three days a week, to the Queens office for her training. Afterward, when she returned she would give me some additional training. They wanted me to learn all the aspects of a payroll administrator. Once my training was finished, they would have no need to use an acting clerk.

The manager then explained to me that the woman whom they were sending to Queens would not be happy once she finds out that she would no longer be used as acting clerk. That I would be working side by side with our Title Grade Three Clerk. Meanwhile, she is in the Queens office. But eventually she will be in this office.

My manager smiled again at me and asked how that sounded to me. I replied, "Just fine." She said, "Now, get the hell out of my office and go home and report back tomorrow. Be ready to work when you get here."

I left for home feeling like I had just won a million dollars sweepstakes. I knew what Mrs. Pumeria had just done was not because she loved me or wanted to help me. Word had come down from higher ups in Albany because I had reported them to the State Board.

That night, I slept better than I had slept since the attack (with the aid of sleeping medication, of course). The next morning when I walked into the office, for the first time in my life, I experienced deep prejudice, hatred, hostility, and maliciousness. This was worse than I had experienced on my first return after my attack. The office I worked in had all black managers. There were no white managers. Out of about three hundred on the payroll, there were only about ten whites in the entire office and they were all operators.

The word was out that I was to start training as the grade three clerk. Therefore, the other operators hated me for that, especially the one who were to train me. Being from the deep south, I had never experienced or faced this type of hate. Black people usually looked out for one another. I now felt like this is worse than hell, and I had never been there. I had a hard time trying to adjust to this type of hatred.

Over the next few weeks while I was in training, I tried very hard to ignore the sly words and loud talk from my new trainer. I knew this was all a ploy for her to cause me to want to leave. One day, Ms. Murphy did not waste any time letting me know that she did not want me at the clerk's desk. She would refer to the desk as her desk.

I was careful not to fight with her. The pens and the pencils, she said, were hers, too. She would also tell me that the clerk's training manual was her book. Sometimes, she even went so far as to hide the books from me and to hide many important sheets of material that she knew I needed to read. She made my life a living hell, but she would never know it because I refused to let on to anyone how hurt I was.

I could never find the employees' time sheets. Without them, I could not enter their hours in for the week. It was important because, otherwise, they would not have a paycheck on Thursdays. Many days, Ms. Murphy would take the time sheets and lock them in her personal locker. I bent over backward trying to get along with her. I did not want a confrontation with her, and I sure did not want to complain about another co-worker to the managers.

I would bite my tongue, smile, and speak politely to try to show her that I was not trying to take anything away from her. I just needed to stay there only until my service pension were bridged, and then I would be out of there. The more I tried to be friendly toward her, the more she would give me nasty remarks. She would never know the pain she was causing me, because I would not let her see me cry. I would not sink down to her level because I had more dignity than that. Plus, I was a Christian and she was not.

I am not bragging, but I just was not going to wallop in dirt because she had no control over my life. There was nothing she could say to me that would cause me to act stupid on the job. As time went by, I would run into the bathroom because of the evil things she would do to me. She wanted a verbal fight. So one day, she pushed on me. I left early that day, thinking it was the best thing to do under the circumstances.

I knew I had to love her regardless of her mistreatment of me. If I complained about her, I knew that would only cause more hostility. One day, I had no choice but to report her because she had taken all of the books and I could not do any work without them. I did not report her to the managers but called the union because, not only was she the acting clerk on light duty as I was, she was also the office union person.

Therefore, after I called the union to report her, she became even worse. I finally made it through training after a few weeks. I had learned more than she had because I had help from a longtime grade three clerk who I had met earlier at that other company. Whenever I had a problem and was not sure, I would call her and she would explain things clearly to me.

One day while I was entering the employees' time for the week, my manager walked over to me. She said, "The other managers had been talking about the good job you have been doing and how you have learned all this in-house much better than the ones who had been sent to the training school."

The appraisal she gave me was very good, so I thanked her and kept on inputting the payroll into the computer. Since it was already late going in, I did not have time for a long conversation. This was the first time in almost eighteen months since my attack that I felt like a real person again.

I was beginning to feel like I was earning that paycheck that I cashed every Thursday morning. Although my pain was worse, I was trying to deal with it by still doubling up on the medication. Many times, I felt as if I was floating on air, but I never made any mistakes on my entry of the employees' time sheets.

It seemed as if the more pain pills I popped the better my performance got. Things were going very good by this time. The employees had calmed down because they finally realized that it was up to me if they received a paycheck every Thursday or not. And if they really got me too upset, they just might not receive their forty hours or I just might forget that they had worked overtime that week. This was the only thing I believe made them start back to being nice to me.

Weeks had passed and one Monday morning as soon as I arrived at the office, my manager said that the office was moving. She said that I needed to start packing up everything. She said that we would have to work out of boxes until they moved us.

She said not to leave any boxes in the central office due to a fire hazard condition, but all the other boxes must be packed and stacked up in the storage room, which was not a very large room.

Therefore, I started packing supplies, books, and everything that I could pack for the move. Every day, I would fill another box and have some of the men in the office lift them on top of each other. Eventually, the storage room was full to capacity.

There was not enough space to walk or just enough space for one person to squeeze through.

One day, a building inspector showed up without warning. He walked into the storage room without being noticed. I was not at my desk nor was the manager in her office. Someone had to have allowed him to enter the building, otherwise, he could not have come up to our floor.

He said that the boxes had to ship out without delay because they were a fire hazard. He said that the company was breaking the law with so many piled up in such a small space. Mrs. Pumeria almost panicked. She asked me why I did not look for her before I let the inspector into the room. I explained to her that I was not at my desk, either. Therefore, I had no way of stopping him. I did not want to accuse anyone, but I felt that it was someone who was angry with me. Who had allowed the inspector to enter the room? However, I said nothing to anyone of my suspicious.

After the inspector left, nothing changed. Mrs. Pumeria said that the new office was not ready yet, so we could not send the boxes over there and have someone steal all of our supplies and material. Weeks passed and the boxes kept piling up and the storage room had become a little shoe hole with very little squeezing space left.

On my way to work the following day, a very strange feeling came over me. It was like the day of my attack. That little voice was nagging at me. My first thought was to go back home and call in sick. But something inside said, "Go on to work." I did not listen again to that small voice warning me. Instead, I went on to work. And as soon as I entered the office, one of the managers, Mrs. Beverly, walked over to me and said that she needed a binder out of the storage room. She said that it was up on the top shelf.

TERROR OF THE RED PANTS ATTACK ON DORCHESTER ROAD

I asked her, "Could I first please put my bag and other personal things on my desk?" She said, "Yes, but I need that binder now because I have to start my work for the day." After I locked my things in my desk drawer, I followed her into the storage room and squeezed myself around the boxes. She said that the binder she needed was on the top shelf. She was forcing me to climb a ladder to reach it. Never mind that the storage room was already overcrowded with boxes.

She wanted me to climb up on a ladder that she knew was almost impossible for me to do. I was already on restricted duty and was not supposed to do any climbing in the first place. However, her intent was for me not to be going with them to the new office. Therefore, she was waiting for me to refuse to climb the ladder so that she would have a good excuse to fire me. If I had refused to obey a superior, it would have been grounds for suspension. Therefore, I did as she asked me to because she said that if I did not, she would send me home. She was trying to block me by insisting that I climb that ladder.

I did not want her to write me up and lose my pay for the day. I did not want that on my records, so whatever they told me to do, I went along with them because things had been going so well. Since this manager was known for being hard, I did not want to rock the boat.

The Accident on the Job

I climbed up the ladder, knowing I had no choice if I wanted to keep my job. (No employee should ever be put in that type of a position as the one I was put in.) When I reached the top self and reached out to get the binder, the book was very large and heavy. As I was coming back down the ladder, I turned my foot, slipped, and I fell. The ladder moved the scale and I fell backward off the ladder onto the cement floor.

All I could remember was trying to grab and hold onto a box for support, but I could not grab hold of anything. My hands just could not grip it. I thought, "Oh, my God! What has happened to me now?" Then I heard my manager say, "What have I done?" She and another clerk were standing over me as I lay there on the floor.

I could feel nothing. I felt numb all over, and the first thing that entered my mind was that my injured neck was now broken again. I heard someone saying, "Do not move her. The ambulance is on the way. Look in her file and get her husband's number. Call him and ask him to meet us at the hospital."

I remember the dreadful pain I felt all over my body. The pain was running from my head down to my feet just like the pain I felt after my attack. I began to think back to earlier that morning when that small voice was telling me not to come in to work today. Why did I not listen? Minutes later, the EMS workers arrived. They were going to put a brace around my neck but discovered that I was already wearing one. So, they put this long wood board under my body, then lifted me onto the stretcher.

Minutes later, we had arrived at the emergency room of Long Island College Hospital. I did not realize that my manager was riding in the ambulance with me. I knew someone was holding my hand, but being semi-conscious, I had no clue that it was her. The person holding my hand did not speak. They said nothing in the ambulance to me. She said later at the hospital that another manager had called my husband and that he said he would meet us at the hospital.

I could tell by the look on her face that Mrs. Beverly was genuinely concerned because she knew that I was not supposed to be on a ladder reaching up for anything. To tell the truth, I really think she was not concerned for me but was more concerned about losing her job.

I remember she kept trying to assure me that everything was going to be all right and that I should not worry about anything. The doctors hurried in to examine me. They knew of my condition and they were concerned. They wheeled me down the hallway to x-ray, then I was wheeled in the room for a CAT scan and back for more x-rays.

I informed them that I was under the care of a neurologist and could they please contact him for me. Since they knew my condition, they agreed to call him. But they informed me that since he was not on their staff, they were sending another neurologist.

They called my doctor. He informed them that he had a partner working in that hospital and to please give him a call. They did as requested, so my private doctor arrived even before they had admitted me in the hospital. He said that there were no new broken bones. However, a disc in my lower back around my tailbone was damaged from the fall. In addition, I had a concussion and had some injuries to the neck.

I was in severe pain and was very frightened. They finally had to admit me into the hospital. They put me in a private room. I was horrified when they told me that they had not seen anything on the CAT scan and the x-rays, and I started to think back on my previous attack and how the doctors all had misread my tests. Therefore, I questioned them thoroughly and explained to them the past doctors' errors, but they assured me that I had no broken bones this time around.

My husband had arrived while I was in the nuclear room taking those tests. When he came up on the floor to my room, he was just as worried as I was. He wanted to know all about my condition. "Have the doctors told you told the truth this time?" he said, because he did not want any delayed diagnosis this time. The doctors explained to my manager what my condition was and that they had to admit me. She told the hospital staff that she was going back to the office to write her report.

The neurologist came into my room again and said that I would probably be in the hospital for a week, or two at the most, for further observation. He said he would come back the next day and keep close watch on me. My husband was sitting next to my bed. He was in disbelief and angry out of fear, because I had not recovered from the attack.

I was still wearing the collar around my neck and now this had happened. I am laid up again. For how long this time, nobody knows. He stayed there by my bedside most of the night, but left to go home to get some sleep because he had to work the next day.

The next day, I received a telephone call from the head person over the company. It was the big boss. He was calling from the head office. He was sympathetic to my injuries and asked me, "Please, do not sue the company." He said that he would make things right. I said to him that he must put it on paper and make the words plain and easy for me to read. "Please, no fancy small writing that I cannot understand." And he agreed.

A few days had passed and the papers from the company arrived for me to sign them. I read over them very carefully before I signed them. There was nothing about ever discussing the accident, only that I agreed not to sue the company.

The doctors said that my hospital stay would be about two weeks. However, after a week, they said that they felt certain that I was able to go home. Therefore, I was released to go home, but the news that I was given was not good. They said that I would never be able to return to work again. That these new injuries had affected the old injuries and that I would have to go out on disability.

TERROR OF THE RED PANTS ATTACK ON DORCHESTER ROAD

I did not want to go anywhere until the company had bridged my time. I needed to work a few more years before this could happen. I had fought the company tooth and nail to stay on the job. Now the doctors are telling me that I have to go out on disability. I was not pleased at this news, but I knew from the new injuries' impact upon the old ones that I had no choice in the matter.

The Final Episode/Retirement

Weeks later, I started going to physical therapy again. I was getting all types of massages and body rubs because there was not much else they could do for me. My condition, being that I was still wearing the collar from my attack, the massages and body rubs were very painful. At times they were almost unbearable because of all the bruises on my body.

The company seemed to be directing all of their anger toward the wrong person. They were blaming me for falling on their premises. The fall was not my fault. I did not request to go up on that ladder. The manager told me to go up or go home.

They said that those boxes in the storage room should not have been in there for so long. I said, "Blame your managers. They were the ones who had me pack them to capacity. So, why are you angry with me? Put the blame where it belongs. On your managers." They called me to ask all sorts of dumb questions. I would tell them, "Stop calling me and speak to your managers."

Had I known this before I signed those papers stating that I would not sue the company and had I known that I would never be able to work again, I would not have signed them. I would have gotten a lawyer and sued them. Therefore, as the weeks went by, the company had me going to many doctors. So many that I have since lost count of their names. They wanted to hear that I could return to duty, but every doctor they sent me to agree with my doctors. I could never work again and they had to accept that.

They had been trying to send me out on Social Security Disability since my return to duty. Now they are trying to bring me back maybe so they could find some excuse to fire me. They had me going around in circles for a while. Months went by and they still had me steadily running to their doctors and more doctors. It had gotten so bad that I was not only having nightmares about my attack, but nightmares about all of the doctors, too.

It had been almost three years since my last injuries. I spent my days taking long walks, reading, and going to church. On my weekly visits with my psychiatrist, he often took little short walks with me to try to ease some of my fear. I was still frightened from my first attack. He was trying to persuade me to join a group therapy session.

However, I was not sure that I wanted to let the world know about my pain at that time in my life. I was not ready to open up to a group of strangers, because I knew I had to be honest with them and could not hold anything back.

There were some changes that took place during my surgery that I could not reveal to strangers or to anyone else. And I cannot, after all of this time, talk about it, either. That is something that will never be revealed. I don't think a person has to tell all of the painful events in their lives to others.

Because the company could not get any of their own doctors to say that I was able to return to duty, they had to stop running me around all over town. Their last doctor even told my doctors that he knew that I was permanently and totally disabled for life.

Therefore, I called my union and they gave me a list of attorneys who handle the employee's worker compensation cases. And since my injury occurred on the job, it fell under the State Workers Compensation Board. The company no longer could intimidate me. It was now in the attorney's hand and I had someone to speak for me. I no longer spoke for myself, and the harassment stopped.

I was still on the payroll while the case was in the courts. But none of the managers called to see how I was doing. They had been calling before, trying to harass me. I figured they just did not care one way or the other.

Finally, on June 6, 1993, the judge closed my case. Thinking back now, I should have sued them right away instead of signing those papers.

However, before I retired, the company was downsizing. People who had more than twenty years of service and I fell into that category. Therefore, I could finally retire under their five and five deal they were offering, so they bridged my service. I was more than happy to take the deal because that's what I had been fighting so hard to get. I took the retirement package and retired with twenty-eight years of service.

I had only been retired for a few weeks when I flew to Birmingham, Alabama, in search of a new home. The search was not a long one because I knew what I wanted. Within a couple of weeks, I had found the ideal home for my husband and I. He flew down to look at the house and agreed that this was the home for us. He flew back to New York while I stayed, and a week later, closed the deal.

After closing the deal, I flew back to New York and packed up everything we had. I was afraid to go anywhere in the city alone. Before the end of August, I was finally on my way out of New York after more than thirty years. My husband came down in November to join me.

My psychiatrist (Dr. Kleinman) thought this was a very good idea because of the fear. He said, being around family members might help me in the long run. Living in the same building was not good therapy for me. And as long as I remained there, I would never stop having the nightmares.

The move was good for me, but the nightmares are still with me today. I think about my attack often. Sometimes I really do think a person never gets over something so tragic. But I also have found out that we can live with the aftereffects of it. Anytime I read that someone has been attacked, I squirm inside because the fear has never left me. I still have the scars to look at every day.

When asked to serve on jury duty, I just cannot because I have no mercy for people who attack and steal from others. I would be prejudiced against the perpetrator.

(All of the names of the people in this book have been changed. I thought it would be better if their real names remain undisclosed.)

I have learned how to forgive people when they hurt me. However, I still have a problem with lazy people who do not want to work and who sit around all day and think of ways to take from others. These types of people, I have no mercy for. I would find them guilty beyond a shadow of doubt without even hearing all of the evidence.

It is hard for me adjusting to only going to church, going shopping, and not being able to play sports again. I pray that someday before I leave this world, I will again be able to pick up a bowling ball. Just to see it roll down the alley once will make me happy.

I hope this book will be a comfort to those who have experienced similar experiences as I have. In addition, remember, we must learn how to forgive and move on because if we do not, the anger will eat us up inside. I am slowly getting there after many years.

We will never realize how blessed we are to have the use of our limbs and how important speech is to us. Moreover, how important it is to have people visit you when you are powerless. It is important to have people in your life who are a positive influence on you. We cannot live in this world alone because we need each other to survive. We are not an island nor do we live in a bubble. People need people to survive.

The feelings that I now have from those traumatic days in Brooklyn, New York, are just as real today as they were then. The thought of that day, June 28, 1990, still sends chills down my spine. But I have learned how to deal with it now. I did not learn this overnight. It took time, and time is all we have to deal with our problems.

My speech did not return back to normal as the speech therapist said. There are times when my words get so muddled until I get choked. People are always trying to help me say what they think I am trying to say. I have had some people walk away from me while I am yet trying to get my words out. Some people can be so mean and rude. They do not understand that I need to speak for myself.

When I explain to them about my attack and how at one point I could not speak at all, pity comes on their faces. "Oh, you poor dear," they say." I do not need their pity because I have lost enough already. So, let me keep my self-respect, please, and you keep your pity to yourselves.

When I think back to my accident on the job, if I had to do it all over again, I would have not climbed that ladder. I think that I would take the suspension and just said no. For years, I have experienced negative feelings, guilt, resentment, anger, and humiliation. I should have had more fight in me. However, during that time, I was still weak and in pain from the attack. I did not want to fight with my managers. All I wanted was to retire with my service pension.

I followed all of the rules, yet the company caused me a lot of pain. Regardless of my manager's motives, she was wrong to insist that I climb that ladder. When people have earned a title as manager, they soon forget the little people under them. Those same people you left while moving up, they will be around to see you coming back down. Therefore, managers do not forget those people at the bottom and never get so high and mighty because limbs on trees break all the time. Sometimes when they fall, they fall hard and break as they hit the bottom.

A Message to All Victims of Vicious Crimes and Attacks

Worldwide, we are bound together by pain, suffering, nightmares, and the senseless acts of violence that have been waged upon us. It is when we suffer, we do not suffer alone because we suffer as one. When we are in pain, that pain seems so unbearable and it will be at times. Just pick up this book and read it again. And when you feel as if you can no longer deal with your situation, do not give up. Take a look around you, and if able, go visit a hospital, nursing home, or better still, go visit your local Veterans Hospital. You will always find someone there with a worse condition than yours.

If you want to feel sorry for yourself, go ahead and do so, because feeling this way is a natural healing remedy especially after an awful attack. After all, your body has been attacked. Don't give other people the chance to feel this way for you. Never allow anyone to tell you to stop feeling the way you do. When you feel the need to scream, start screaming as loud as you can. This is also a part of your healing, and you need to release the tension. I found early on that the more and louder I screamed, the better I felt when it was over.

We are wounded warriors, and we are one. However, do not spend forever feeling like a wounded warrior because that would not be healthy. We each know our limits and our length of mourning. Anytime we lose any part of our body that can no longer function, we must mourn that loss. Mourn because you have lost something that was dear to you. However, the mourning has to end at some point, because if it doesn't, you will never move past it to heal.

We have a community of victims who can all share in our life stories. As it is with any victim of a crime, they never get a chance to express themselves the way they ought to. Some are too ashamed to talk about it, while others will never seek the professional help that they need.

I spent five years in therapy after my attack, because I needed help and I got it. This book will be of great help and comfort to you, the readers. Read it, tell your love one, your friends, your neighbors, and your church members about it. Tell them to go out and purchase their own copy because yours is your daily word.

Invite people on your job, in your shopping center, and at the grocery store to read my story. Tell everyone you know about this book. This is also the good news as I see it because people need to hear how I survived a double tragedy.

There were many people who tried to break my spirit and tear me down. But through it all, God would not let them. I'm here today because of my faith in God and my persistence to keep moving forward because, when man said go home and rest, my God said keep going, your answer is in those x-rays.

Therefore, I say to all victims: do not give up because your answer to what you need to know is in your spiritual x-rays. Look inside for them.

Thank you for listening to me through my book about my story.

The Statistics of Doctors Errors

From the Wikipedia Report

The examples, and perspective in this article deal primary with the United States and not worldwide. It is estimated that 142,000 people died in 2013 from adverse effects of medical treatment. This an increase from 94,000 in 1990. However, a 2016 study of the number of deaths that were a result of medical error in the United States placed the yearly death rate in the U.S. along at 251,452 deaths, which suggests that the 2013 global estimation may not be accurate.
This ends this report.
Unfortunately, doctors' misdiagnosis isn't as common as I was misdiagnosed four times.
Are statistics alarming? Look back at 1990 when I was attacked to see how many have died since then?

> National Medical Malpractice Statistics
> Statistics Profile of Medical Malpractice

Patients 60% female-ages 38
One-fifth Newborns

Twelve percent over sixty-five years of age—numbers are from 2006, New England Journal of Medicine Study. I took a random look at 1,452 resolved Medical Malpractice cases involving Malpractice

Insurance carriers across all regions of the United States. Average Compensation in Medical Malpractice claims settlements through Jury awards from 2005–2009.

The study appeared in Journey of American Medical Association (JAMA), average compensation for Medical Malpractice occurred in the inpatient setting was around $363,000, while average award for health care mistakes outpatient setting was $290,000. Results of the NEJM study claims $485,000. Average jury awards after a verdict in court checking twice average $799,000. Jury awards $ 462,000 settlement.

Most common reasons—errors in diagnosis made up about 46% all medical malpractice dates from the JAMA study mentioned above, according to the 2009 Congressional Budget office report, total direct costs insurance settlements and awards and administration cost. Not covered by insurance was $35 billion in 2009. This figure represented 2% of the total healthcare expenditures across the United Stated for that same year.

This ends this report.

Medical errors rank as the number three killer in the United States, claiming 250,000 lives annually. Medical errors claim the lives of roughly 685 Americans per day.

This ends this report.

The study appeared in *Journal of American Medical Association* (JAMA), average compensation for Medical Malpractice occurred in the inpatient setting was around $363,000 while average award for health care mistakes outpatient setting was $290,000, while results of the NEJM study claims $485,000. Average jury awards after a verdict in court checking twice average $799,000. Jury awards $ 462,000 settlement.

Most common reasons—errors in diagnosis made up about 46% all medical malpractice, dates from the JAMA study mentioned above. According to the 2009 Congressional Budget office report, total direct costs insurance settlements and awards and administration cost. Not covered by insurance was $35 billion in 2009. This figure represented 2% of the total healthcare expenditures across the United Stated for that same year.

TERROR OF THE RED PANTS ATTACK ON DORCHESTER ROAD

This ends this report.

DC Medical Malpractice and Patient Safety Blog
Published by Patrick Malone Associations 5-5-2015

Medical errors rank as the number three killer in the United States claiming 250,000 lives annually. Medical errors claim the lives of roughly 685 Americans per day.
This ends this report.

Hospitals Mistakes
Pictures Taken while in Hospital to All Victims
Hospitals Visited
Caledonia 6 /28/20 3:55p.m. /Diagnosis/ Soft Tissue Injury/ Discharged-5:35 p.m.
K.C. H. 6/28/90-11:35p.m. / Diagnosis/ Soft Tissue Injury/ Discharged/ 4:35 a.m.
6/29/90
H.M.C. 6/30/90
Kingsboro Medical Center 7/90
Company Medical Center 7/90
H.M.C. 7/70
Long Island City Hospital 7/26/93/ Discharged 7/31/93

Doctors Visited
Dr. J. Noh
Dr. Irving Friedman
Dr. Stuart Klienman
Dr. N. Derman
Dr. A. Battista
Dr. Allan Perel
Dr. Sam Chwat, Ms., c.c.c.-Sp./ New York Speech Improvement Services
Dr. R. Hamlin
Dr. Robbins
Dr. Weber
Dr. Schwarcz

About the Author

Nancy Seay is married to Elijah, and on October fourth 2016, they will celebrate forty-five years of bliss. She is a seventy-year old mother of one son, David, one stepdaughter Tracey, one stepson Marlon, three granddaughters Somolia, Damany, and Keonijah, two stepgranddaughters, Ashley and Brianna, and one great-grandson, Jah'aire.

She is a graduate of Bethel Divinity College and Seminary.

She attended City College-Brooklyn, New York.

She worked for a communications company from 1971–1996 and retired from that company in August 1996. She returned to her home in Birmingham, Alabama.

This is my first book about my own tragic story. My name is Nancy Seay and I am a native of Alabama. I was born the second of eight children.

I began my formal education in the public schools of Westfield, Alabama, which is a steel town owned by the United States Steel Company.

I moved to New York in the early sixties. I attended The City College-Brooklyn, New York, with a major in marketing management and sales..

I have worked as a salesperson on three different jobs. My most profitable one was when I worked for (Borough President Andrew Stein's wife) at The Pay Telephone Company. This was outside groundbreaking door-to-door sales. The other two were inside sales.

I spent the bulk of my career working for a communications company. I earned my Bachelor of Arts and my Master of Ministry from Bethel Divinity and Seminary.

I am married and will celebrate forty-five years of bliss this October. I'm a seventy-year-old mother of one son, one stepdaughter, one stepson, three granddaughters, two step granddaughters, and one great-grandson.

Dennis Duggan, writer for the New York Post, interviewed me five months before my attack on Tuesday, January 16, 1990. We (my church) were getting ready to march across the Brooklyn Bridge to City Hall. It was Dr. Martin L. King's Celebration Day.

I played on the company's softball team in the early eighties. Our last game, we beat the New Jersey team 50 to 5. I was the catcher. I was a volunteer working with the New York City Handicapped Children. We would take them on outings on my days off. I also was a volunteer working with the New York City Blood Bank (on my job).

As a writer, I will have the benefit of discussing in detail the tragic events that occurred on June 28, 1990. I will tell in detail how the attacker robbed and assaulted me and left me for dead, as well as how my attacker put his gun to my head but it jammed.

Two different hospitals and four doctors misdiagnosed my injuries. They told me that my x-rays only showed soft tissue injuries and that my collarbone was sprained.

Two of the four doctors said that the majority of the pain was in my head. I was the only one who knew that the pain was not all in my bead. The feelings in my left arm were gone, as was the left side of my face. I could not put words together to form a sentence. The speech was incoherent. They were just blabber and jitter. I could no longer walk on my left foot and was tipping around on my left toes. Only the right foot was touching the ground.

I would not give up or give in to the idea that it was in my head. God kept me going from doctor to doctor for more than three weeks in this painful partially paralyzed condition. One day, I just refused to leave the doctor's office until I was told why I was becoming paralyzed. I made it very clear to him that he must look at my tests again.

Seeing the look on my face and the tears in my eyes, this doctor knew I was serious. Therefore, he agreed to look at the films again. After looking this time, he picked up his telephone and dialed another doctor. His words were, "Doctor, I have a patient sitting here in my office who you need to see right away. This is an emergency. I will put them (my husband and I) in a taxi and send them right away."

When we arrived in lower Manhattan, the doctor was a surgeon. He looked at me and then asked my husband, "How long has your wife been walking around in all this pain? She is lucky to be alive," he said. "I cannot figure out how she is still alive all this time." He took the films that the doctor had sent with us and looked at them and said, "Her neck is broken and the bone is almost through the skin in her back. It is a miracle she is still alive."

This book is a powerful, triumphant true story of motivation, faith, and determination. How I was motivated even when doctors said the pain was all in my head. I kept seeking and moving when many days I was almost to the point of crawling. This tells how other people can move when the pain tells them don't. I show through my own struggles that nothing is impossible if you do not give up.

I show them step by step how to be g persuasive, how to take no for an answer (which will improve their lives), and how set backs can lead to set-ups. This book contain pertinent information that will reach all audiences because in every family, in every house, in every state and country, people all over the world will have a doctor to tell them, "I find nothing wrong with you." Maybe a friend or a loved one has died from a misdiagnosis. Doctors looked but did not see the problem. People have died from being misinformed.

There have been too many people assaulted who cannot seem to move on with their lives. This book will give them the motivation to move ahead when they feel that the odds are against them. This book will reach all ages because of the crime that is going on in our world today.

The content of this book will make it easy for readers to find what they are looking for in the book. Since I lived through this experience when some people thought I would die, this makes me more than qualified to write such a book. Not many people can walk around for more than three weeks with a broken neck and live to write about it.

Too many people give up without knowing what is wrong with them. In addition, some die and family members never know the truth. Therefore, people need a book like this. This book will make its readers stop and think.

No one has published a book such as this one because I am the only one who knows all the facts. In comparison to other books in this genre, my book will succeed as those and over. I am positive that this is going to be a best-seller and a movie will be made about it. If I seem to be over confident, well I am, because I did not wait more than twenty years to write a flop.

CPSIA information can be obtained
at www.ICGtesting.com
Printed in the USA
BVOW08s1750140417
481276BV00001B/3/P